PSYCHOLOGY RESEARCH PROGRESS

BEHAVIORAL ECONOMIC ANALYSIS OF THE SELF

PSYCHOLOGY RESEARCH PROGRESS

Additional books in this series can be found on Nova's website
under the Series tab.

PSYCHOLOGY RESEARCH PROGRESS

BEHAVIORAL ECONOMIC ANALYSIS OF THE SELF

SHINJI TERAJI

Nova Science Publishers, Inc.
New York

For permission to use material from this book please contact us:
Telephone 631-231-7269; Fax 631-231-8175
Web Site: http://www.novapublishers.com

LIBRARY OF CONGRESS CATALOGING-IN-PUBLICATION DATA

Teraji, Shinji.
Behavioral economic analysis of the self / Shinji Teraji.
p. cm.
Includes bibliographical references and index.
ISBN 978-1-61209-551-6 (softcover)
1. Economics--Psychological aspects. 2. Self--Economic aspects. I. Title.
HB74.P8T47 2011
330.01'9--dc22

2010054267

Published by Nova Science Publishers, Inc. † New York

CONTENTS

PREFACE

This book reviews the recent behavioral economic literature on the "self." First, we view intertemporal choice as the outcome of a conflict between multiple selves. The behavioral implications of imperfect self-control by a single decision maker are examined. Discounting does not occur by a fixed rate per unit of time, and instead occurs in a way that implies dynamic inconsistency. Self-control phenomena can be predicted by hyperbolic discounting. The consumption behavior of hyperbolic consumers sets up a conflict between the preferences of different intertemporal selves. Second, we discuss identity in economics. Identity is a person's sense of self.Multiple categories and attributes represent how an individual views himself / herself, and are likely to have different weights to the sense of self. An individual identity describes gains and losses in utility from behavior that conformsor departs from the norms for particular social categories in particular situations. Third, we discuss possible selves in economics, and consider how intentional self-change occurs. The self-system is multifaceted and dynamic, with different self-representations activated at different times. Comparison between the actual self and the ideal self has important motivational consequences.Lastly, we examine the evolutionary emergence of social preferences in the long run. Economic behavior can be described as either altruistic or envious.Conformity with social normswill be self-enforcing in the presence of multiple equilibria. There are situations in which other-regarding preferences may dominate the outcome of social interactions.

Grateful acknowledgement is due to the Japan Society for the Promotion of Science (JSPS) and Yamaguchi Cable Vision Co., Ltd. (C-able) for their financial support.

Chapter 1

INTRODUCTION

What is the "behavioral" in behavioral economics? The word "behavioral" emphasizes that this aims to study how flesh-and-blood people act. Actual decisions involve some error. The economist's basic picture of preferences, beliefs, and rationality has been subject to challenges from empirical anomalies. Behavioral economics encourages economists to be more receptive to the results of experimental research. By adding insights from psychology, behavioral economics tries to modify the standard economic approach. The idea of behavioral and cognitive modularity helps explicate a variety of otherwise anomalous observations.

Since the early 1970s, the psychologists Daniel Kahneman and Amos Tversky published a series of articles testing the standard economic model of choice under uncertainty. In their early research, people rely on a limited number of heuristic principles which reduce the complex tasks of assessing probabilities and predicting values to simpler judgmental operations (Kahneman and Tversky, 1974).These heuristics usually work well, but in some contexts they lead to severe and systematic errors. [1] Prospect theory(Kahneman and Tversky, 1979) is, without any doubt, the most influential one. The theory suggests that choices depend on the framing of a problem. Our perceptual apparatus is attuned to the evaluation of changes

[1] There are three heuristics: representativeness, availability, and anchoring (Kahneman and Tversky, 1974). The representative heuristic captures the idea that probabilities are evaluated by the degree to which an event or object is representative of a class of events or objects. Availability derives from the hypothesis that people assess the probability of an event by the rate or ease with which instances or occurrences can be brought to mind. Anchoring is based on the observation that people solve problems by starting from an initial guess or salient starting point that is then adjusted to generate a final answer.

rather than to the evaluation of absolute magnitudes. People tend to privilege the "status quo" (their current position) and are sensitive to changes from the status quo. In prospect theory, utility is assigned to changes from a reference point which may be the status quo. The reference point determines whether something is entered as gains or losses on the mental ledger. Its S-shaped "value function" shows changes (gains and losses) in material well-being on the horizontal axis and happiness resulting from these changes on the vertical axis. The S-shape displays diminishing marginal sensitivity to both gains and losses. Furthermore, the loss function is steeper than the gain function("loss aversion").To capture loss aversion, the value function is assumed to have a kink at the reference point. Prospect theory was explicitly presented as a formal descriptive theory of the choices that people actually make.

Psychologists distinguish between two kinds of theories: normative and descriptive (Thaler, 2000). Normative theories characterize rational choices (the axioms of expected utility theory). Descriptive theories, meanwhile, try to characterize actual choices. Prospect theory is an example of a descriptive theory. Psychologists hypothesize that subjects make systematic errors by using heuristics and make systematic forecast errors by using adaptive rather than rational expectations. Economists often criticize psychological research for its propensity to generate lists of errors and biases, and for its failure to offer a coherent alternative to rational-agent model (Kahneman, 2003). Economic agents have beliefs which are the probabilities (they think) various outcomes will occur conditional on available information. Rationality is the extent to which economic agents succeed in choosing optimal actions in the light of their beliefs. Higher cognitive abilities do not universally govern behavior. Although psychological theories cannot match the elegance and precision of normative theories, rational-agent models are psychologically unrealistic. Decision-making errors are both widespread and predictable.Furthermore, as emphasized by Kahneman (2003), psychologists have long recognized the distinction between System 1 (quick and intuitive) and System 2 (reasoned and deliberate).[2] System 1 closely corresponds to automatic (and often emotionally charged) processing governed by habit; it quickly proposes intuitive answers to problems as they arise. System 2 closely corresponds to deliberately controlled processes (potentially rule-governed); it

[2] Psychology has two main branches: cognitive and behavioral (Gintis, 2007). The former defines the brain as an "information-processing organ" and generally argues that humans are relatively poor, irrational, and inconsistent decision makers. The latter is preoccupied with learning mechanisms that humans share with virtually all metazoans (stimulus response, the law of effect, operant, conditioning, and the like).

monitors the quality of answers provided by System 1 and, in some situations, corrects and overrides these judgments.

Economists usually describe likes and dislikes as preferences. The behavioral economic approach challenges conventional accounts of the content and origins of human preferences.One of the key messages of behavioral economics is that context matters in ways that are not recognized in standard economic modeling. For example, context matters for the tradeoff between current and future concerns. The individual's motivations in the standard economic model are described by a preference relation (or a utility function) over all potentially available alternatives. Among the available alternatives, the individual selects the one that he/she ranks the highest. Explaining behavior involves describing how changes in various environmental factors affect the optimal choice. Behavior can vary with elements of the description that play no role in the usual formulation. A consumer's taste for immediate gratification leads him / her to systematically overconsume harmful products and underconsume beneficial ones. There are fundamental limitations in the market's ability to provide consumers with self-control.

The primary contribution of the behavioral approach to economics is to understand the diversity and context-dependent nature of human preferences, how elements of this repertoire of preferences become salient in particular strategic interactions, how they have evolved over the long run, and how individuals form the beliefs that along with their preferences explain what people do (Bowles and Gintis, 2000).Although Adam Smith's *Theory of Moral Sentiments*, published in 1759, starts from assumptions about human nature (in modern language, from assumptions about human psychology), it is presented as a contribution to social theory rather than as an investigation of individual psychology (Sugden, 2005).In *The Theory of Moral Sentiments*, Smith argued that behavior was determined by the struggle between the myopic "passions"and far-sighted "impartial spectator."Smith (1759 [1976]) viewed sympathy as one of the more important passions though he argued that it often falls short of what is morally required.The impartial spectator plays an essential role in fairness, by causing individuals to internalize others' sense of fairness. The impartial spectator perspective, which derives from sympathy, becomes operational to evaluate, to control, and to restructure our behavior.The conventional neoclassical hypothesis of the economic agent as a creature driven by material self-interest has provided powerful theoretical tools in the analysis of diverse problems. However, this self-interest hypothesis biases the analytical predictions of economic theory in an unreasonable and unrealistic fashion that runs contrary to the stylized facts of economic behavior. In fact, experimental support for the narrow conventional hypothesis has been fragile. One of the important experimental games that eventually led many economists to realize the self-interest hypothesis is problematic was the "ultimatum game"by Güth, Schmittberger, and Schwarze (1982).[3] Furthermore, recent neuroeconomic studies support the view that people derive non-pecuniary utility from mutual cooperation, despite strong free-riding incentives, and from punishing norm violators (Fehr, Fischbacher, and Kosfeld, 2005).Neuroeconomics provides a "microfoundation" for individual beliefs, preferences, and behavior by examining the brain processes associated with the formation of beliefs, the perception of the action set, and the actual choice. This means that subjects' feelings for others can be measured in terms of brain activity, not limited to measurement by self-reports or by making inferences about their motives from observed behavior.

How closely we wish to interweave economics with psychology depends both on the range of questions we wish to answer and on our assessment of how far we may trust the assumptions of static equilibrium as approximations (Simon, 1959). Simon coins the term "bounded rationality" to refer to rational choices given the physiological cognitive limitations on the individual decision makers in terms of acquiring and processing of information. He takes it as an axiom; human beings are capable only of very approximate and bounded rationality. Human beings do not know all of the alternatives that are available for action, and they are unable to make the calculations that would support optimization.Decision making that deviates from neoclassical rationality does not imply irrationality or even errors or biases.

It is common in neoclassical economics to assume that effort is maximized in its quantity and quality dimensions irrespective of institutional conditions. However, Harvey Leibenstein's theory of x-efficiency poses a problem for studies of effort variability and emphasizes the importance of

[3] In an ultimatum game, there is a fixed sum of money and one player, the "proposer," makes a take-it-or-leave-it offer of how to divide the amount between himself / herself and another person. If the second person, the "responder,"accepts the division, then both players get the specified division. If the responder rejects it, they both receive nothing. If the responder is self-interested, he / she will accept any offer. If the proposer anticipates this and cares only about how much money he / she gets, he / she will offer the smallest amount of money. In experiments, however, proposers offer between 40 and 50 percent of the money and responders reject small offers of 20 percent or so half the time. Many responders do not behave in a self-interest maximizing manner. Dictator games are ultimatum games with the responder's ability to reject the offer removed. In Kahneman, Knetsch, and Thaler (1986), subjects were given a choice between dictating an even split of a fixed amount of money with another person, or an uneven split favoring themselves. Three-quarters chose the equal split.

interaction between patterns of production and worker morale (Leibenstein, 1987). X-efficient production represents the maximum level of output that can be realized by utility-maximizing agents. According to the theory of x-efficiency, effort is a discretionary variable in the production process and is affected by the environment. X-inefficiency can be defined as differences in productivity between what can be achieved when economic agents supply effort in an ideal environment and what is supplied in a sub-optimal environment.Economic agents are not all the same and therefore characterized by different objective functions. Whether x-efficiency is achieved or not depends on the economic agents' preferences. According to Simon (1978), responses to environmental events can no longer be predicted simply by analyzing the "requirements of the situation," but depend on the specific decision processes that the agent employs. If, in the face of identical environmental conditions, different decision mechanisms can produce important consequences for analysis at the level of markets and the economy.

Simon (1993) supposes that human choice is driven by a number of motives, not limited to economic gain, that are based on anticipated consequences (pleasure and pain) for the chooser.[4] He argues that human beingsdo not behave optimally for their fitness. Because of bounded rationality, individuals have a tendency to act on advice and respect norms. Then, "docility" contributes to the fitness of human beings in evolutionary competition. Here, docility means the tendency to depend on suggestions, recommendations, persuasion, and information obtained through social channels as a major basis for choice.

As Simon (1993) points out,

> "In large measure, we do what we do because we have learned from those who surround us, not from our own experience, what is good for us and what is not. Behaving in this fashion contributes heavily to our fitness because (a) social influences will generally give us advice that is "for our own good" and (b) the information on which this advice is based is far better than the information we could gather independently. As a consequence, people exhibit a very large measure of docility. On average, it contributes to their fitness and hence drives out nondocility in evolutionary competition."(1993,p.157)

[4] Kaufman (1999) suggests that Simon's concept of bounded rationality could be extended and enriched by a more explicit incorporation of emotions. Emotions can play a more positive role, for example, in motivating agents by raising the saliency of certain desires, wants, and outcomes.

Simon claims that successful human societies are ones where docility is psychologically associated with altruism so that the net gain to individuals from docility is positive. Docile persons often make choices that reduce their own fitness under social advice to do so. Certain kinds of common understandings among individuals are then required to produce the common associations of ideas that allow conventions to emerge and to reproduce themselves. Social interaction will lead individuals to behave in a more similar manner. Vernon Smith (2003) develops the concept of a rational order as an undesigned ecological system that emerges out of cultural and biological evolutionary processes. "Ecological rationality" uses reason to discover the possible intelligence embodied in the rules, norms, and institutions of our cultural and biological heritage that are created from human interactions but not by deliberate human design. People follow rules without being able to articulate them, but they can be discovered. Furthermore, social norms are often considered to be the historical legacy of a traditional culture supported and adhered to in a population.

There are many economic phenomena that cannot be explained without an understanding of social norms.Cultural conformity occurs when individuals are more likely to share variants of a cultural trait with others. Individual behavior is motivated largely by social factors. Social groups often penalize individuals who deviate from social customs by loss of social "reputation" (Akerlof, 1980). Akerlof (1997) also presents a model of social distance. The social distance approach incorporates sociological insights into individual decision making. Akerlof argues that concerns for status and conformity are key drivers of individual outcomes.In social space, people try to move themselves closer to everyone else. In the conformist model, he / she embeds a desire to conform (or an aversion for social distance) directly into the utility function; utility declines as distance between the individual's choice and that of everyone else increases.The individual wants to minimize the social distance between himself / herself and others. In Bernheim (1994), status is assumed to depend on public perceptions about individuals' predispositions rather than on the individuals' actions (how others perceive them). Individuals care not only about their intrinsic preferences but also about status. They are willing to conform because they recognize that behavioral departures from the social norm will impair their status. We are then careful in what follows to recognize beliefs and norms of others.

The standard economic model of individual decision making is based on three concepts: the action set, preferences, and beliefs. The individual maximizes stable and coherent preferences given rational beliefs. Utility maximization is then thought of as a goal. However, to maximize utility successfully, a person must start by making a forecast about how various possible outcomes will be experienced (Kahneman and Thaler, 2006). If forecasts are systematically biased, then choices may systematically fail to maximize utility.

People confront a wide range of choices that involve the tradeoffs between current and future rewards. Evaluations can be made over different dates. The theory of discounted utility provides a framework for evaluating delayed rewards. The standard theory assumes that an individual's preferences over the alternatives available at some future date don't change as the date approaches. However, many experiments document that people suffer from present bias. People appear to have dynamically inconsistent preferences. Psychological research teaches us about ways to describe preferences more realistically, about biases in belief-formation, and about ways it is misleading to conceptualize people as attempting to stable, coherent, and accurately perceived preferences (Rabin, 1998). Behavioral economics also pursues policy implications. Insights from behavioral economics may change existing policy analyses.

The behavioral economic approach demonstrates that rewards are discounted proportionally with their delay ("hyperbolic discounting"). Hyperbolic discounting implies that the increase in valuation that occurs when moving a fixed unit of time closer to an expected outcome is proportionately greater the closer one is to that outcome (Ainslie, 1975). Impulsive behavior can be found among animals, children, and adults. The standard economic procedure to compare outcomes at different times, introduced by Samuelson (1937), is to discount them at a constant rate and sum them up. The standard economic analysis requires that devaluation occurs as an exponential function of delay. The weight at which future costs and benefits influence today's decisions declines exponentially over time. If delayed outcomes are devalued exponentially, then the relative preference of expected future outcomes does not change as the individual moves closer in time to those outcomes. Exponential discounting preserves time consistency. Time consistency means that the future actions required to maximize the current present value of utility remain optimal in the periods when the actions are to be taken. Unlike exponential discount functions, hyperbolic discount functions predict time inconsistency.The relative valuation of utility flows at different dates changes as the planning date evolves.People have higher discount rates over payoffs in the near future than in the distant future. Individuals are highly impatient about consuming between today and tomorrow but are much more patient about choices advanced further in the future, for example, between 365 and 366 days from now.

In the following chapters, we review the recent behavioral economic literature on the "self."

Chapter 2 viewsintertemporal choice as the outcome of a conflict between multiple selves. A conflict will occur between today's preferences and tomorrow's preferences. Individuals do things they would not have done if they had made the decision to act from a remote perspective, and they do not follow their own plans. The behavioral implications of imperfect self-control by a single decision maker are examined.Hyperbolic discounting transforms a unitary self into a population of competing selves. The self is a dynamic and ever-changing entity over time. Given some sets of alternatives, hyperbolic discounting predicts that an individual will hold preferences that he / she can foresee will be threatened by his / her own future self.Self-control phenomena can be predicted by hyperbolic discounting.

Chapter 3 discusses identity in economics.Akerlof and Kranton (2000) introduce the concept of "identity," in particular a person's social identity, into a standard utility function. They associate identity with the social categories to which an individual belongs. The social categories are linked with particular socially determined "self-images." Individuals identify with people in some categories and differentiate themselves from those in others. The concept of identity depends on a person's own actions as well as on those of others, on one's assigned social categories, and on how well one's own given personal characteristics as well as actions match those of the assigned categories. They present a prototype model with two different social categories (Green and Red) both associated with a particular action. Deviations from the prescription generate disutility. Identity is then the extent to which members of a particular group associate themselves with their background or culture.Standard economic models are based on the methodological individualism that postulates that preferences are strictly personal. Economists often hesitate to incorporate values, norms and more generally cultural aspects.Chapter 3also develops a theory of oppositional cultures. An oppositional culture is a minority of a population with norms and beliefs that differ from the norms and beliefs of the majority. Differences in norms tied to social identities help explain differences in economic outcomes.

Chapter 4 discusses possible selves in economics, and considers how intentional self-change occurs.Possible selves are future-oriented representations of the self that provide context for interpreting and evaluating selves and motivate behavior.[5] The self-system is multifaceted.Distinct selves are typically tied to a particular situation. Furthermore, the self-system is highly dynamic. Self-conceptions can be activated by certain features of the situation. Although people may have distinct multiple selves, only one of them tends to guide behavior.People may perceive, seek out, and create events in such a way to enhance their views of themselves with respect to their environmental surroundings. Weconceptualizethe self that includes self-state representations, the actual self and the ideal self. The ideal self would place principles and values above practical considerations. Comparison between the actual self and the ideal self will have important motivational consequences.

Chapter 5 examines the evolutionary emergence of social preferences in the long run. Geneticists developed the distinction between a genotype and a phenotype. Genotypes are mapped onto phenotypes that have different abilities to survive and reproduce. Herbert Simon claims that successful human societies are ones where docility is psychologically associated with altruism so that the net gain to individuals from docility is positive. Simon defines docility as a willingness to be taught or to defer to the superior knowledge of others. A cultural trait is a belief, value, or other acquired aspect of an individual that influences one's behavior in some durable fashion. Evolutionary models, not based on kinship, demonstrate how altruistic traits, such as Simon calls docility, can have survival values. The relevant traits may be transmitted genetically, or they may be transmitted culturally through social learning and proliferate because successful groups tend to absorb failing groups. In particular, conformity to a norm is conditional on expectations about other peoples' behavior and beliefs. Social dynamics influencing norms are important for understanding how economic behavior is acquired and transmitted in society.The intuition behind complements can be extended to strategic contexts. When choices are complements, then self-regarding (or other-regarding) agents may have an incentive to mimic the behavior of other-regarding (or self-regarding) agents. Therefore, there are situations in which other-regarding (or self-regarding) preferences may dominate the outcome of social interactions. In our formulation, economic behavior can be described as either altruistic or envious.This multiplicity can explain why economic performance varies across societies. Conformity with norms will be self-enforcing in the presence of multiple equilibria.

---

[5] In their seminal presentation of the construct, Markus and Nurius (1986) define possible selves as "self-knowledge that pertains to how individuals think about their potential and about their future."

Our approach uses standard microeconomic theory as a *reference point* for defining rational behavior which, in turn, is identified with intelligent behavior. One aspect of behavioral economics is to understand how cognitive abilities, emotions, culture, and institutions affect intelligent decision-making. Economic theory requires a solid foundation in the psychological, sociological, and institutional underpinnings. One can have rational decisions that are inefficient, sub-optimal, or error-prone. Inefficiencies can be generated by the choices of rational individuals. Each individual can have a different objective function. Our models demonstrate how intelligent human action can determine differences in material payoffs among individuals, firms, and societies.

Chapter 2

TEMPORAL SELVES

2.1. HYPERBOLIC DISCOUNTING

Most people complain that they don't have enough of self-control. Self-control problems exist when a choice is between a currently available good and an option that requires bearing a current cost associated with a deferred benefit. Agents have a tendency to succumb to short-run impulses at the expense of their long-run interests. They tend to overconsume goods that provide an immediate reward but affect negatively their future welfare, through a deterioration of health (drinking, smoking, overeating, etc.) or a decrease in wealth (compulsive credit card purchases, consumption of luxury goods, gambling, etc.). That is, the individual's current self overweighs the present relative to the future.

Intertemporal choices are decisions with consequences that play out over time. The standard economic theory has analyzed intertemporal decision making by using the discounted utility model, which assumes that people evaluate the pleasures and pains resulting from a decision in much the same way that financial markets evaluates the gains and losses. The discounted utility model involves an agent who chooses a feasible consumption plan to maximize his / her present exponentially discounted utility. The critical feature of exponential discounting is that it preserves dynamic consistency. Intertemporal choices are no different from any other type of choices except that some consequences are delayed. Psychologists have questioned the validity of the assumption of exponential discounting on the basis of experimental evidence (Ainslie, 1975; Kirby and Herrnstein, 1995). Events in the near future tend to be discounted at a higher rate than events that occur in the long run. Self-control and procrastination are now topics of growing interests to behavioral economic theorists (Laibson, 1997; O'Donoghue and Rabin, 1999a, 1999b). The behavioral economic approach has criticized the traditional approach suggesting an alternative specification of discounting, that is, hyperbolic discounting.

The reversal of preferences is called time inconsistency. A person may reverse the decisions formulated in the earlier stage. An individual who is offered a choice today of receiving $50 in 100 days or $60 in 101 days will take the$60, but when the options are moved forward, so that he / she can either have the $50 immediately or $60 tomorrow, he / she chooses the $50. Subjects exhibit a reversal of preferences when choosing between a smaller-sooner reward and a larger-later one in experiments. The earlier reward is preferred when it offers an immediate payoff whereas the latter reward is preferred when both rewards are received with delay. Time-inconsistent preferences are proposed by Stroz (1956), and further developed by Phelps and Pollak (1968).[1] Time inconsistency implies that an ex ante optimal decision is not carried out because a latter reevaluation suggests that it is not optimal anymore.

Since Stroz (1956), economists have known that intertemporal choices are time consistent only if agents discount exponentially using a discount rate that is constant over time. People are more impatient when they make short-run tradeoffs than when they make long-run tradeoffs. Hence, the rates of time preferences would be very high in the short run but much lower in the long run, as viewed from today's perspective. The contrast between short-run impatience and long-run patience has been modeled using hyperbolic discounting. Hyperbolic discounting rationalizes the preferences for present consumption as a form of time inconsistency. This creates a conflict between an individual agent's preferences at different points in time. Ainslie (2001) explains violations of delay-independence in terms of the steepness of a function which discounts the utility of a reward.[2] In contrast to exponential discount curves, hyperbolic discount curves depict a strong but temporary tendency to prefer a smaller-sooner reward to a larger-later one, in the period just before the smaller-sooner reward is due. The time-inconsistency approach

[1] "Quasi-hyperbolic" discount functions were introduced by Phelps and Pollak (1968) in a model of imperfect intergenerational altruism.

[2] As suggested by Loewenstein (1987), this steepness is related to several emotional factors that are involved in decisions over time. Some of our emotions are caused by expectations about outcomes, and people have goals concerning these emotions as well as concerning the outcomes themselves.

postulates that people may have a variety of selves that become dominant at different points because of their timing.For example, before the party, one self favors a strict limit of two beers during the evening, but at the party, having already consumed the two beers, the current self feels certain of the desirability of having just one more beer. An agent who discounts rewards hyperbolically is not a straightforward value estimator, but a succession of estimators whose conclusions differ. The hyperbolic discounter is then involved in a decision that has "intrapersonal" strategic dimensions. Individual choices are taken to be the outcome of an intrapersonal game in which the same individual agent is represented by a different player at every date. Intrapersonal games are played among the agent's temporally situated selves. A variety of conflicting reward-getting processes will grow and survive within the individual, sometimes leading to harmful choices in the long run.

In formal discounting models, a consumer's welfare can be represented as a discounted sum of current and future utility. The model assumes that, at each point in time t, the agent consumes goods c_t. The subjective value to the consumer is given by a (instantaneous) utility function $u(c_t)$, which translates the consumption measure, c_t, into a single measure of utility at period t. The discount rate measures the rate of decline of the discount function. The discount function measures the value of utility, as perceived from the present, at each future time period. Exponential discount functions have a constant discount rate. Specifically, a util delayed τ periods is worth δ^{τ} as much as a util enjoyed immediately ($\tau = 0$). Here, δ is assumed to be less than one (future utils are worth less than current utils). Exponential discount functions also have the property that they don't generate preference reversals. For a time-consistent agent, discounted utility at period t takes the familiar form:

$$\sum_{\tau=0}^{\infty} \delta^{\tau} u(c_{t+\tau}). \quad (1)$$

An agent who discounts exponentially maximizes his / her intertemporal utility in expression (1).

Most experimental evidence suggests that the discount rate declines with the length of the delay horizon. When two rewards are both far away in time, people act relatively patiently. But when both rewards are brought forward in time, preferences exhibit a reversal, reflecting more impatience. The actual discount function declines at a greater rate in the short run than in the long run.

The agent behaves given the predicted behavior of his / her subsequent selves. Such discounting patterns play a role in generating self-control problems.[3]

An individual is modeled as a sequence of autonomous temporal selves. Temporal selves indexed by periods $t = 0, 1, 2, \ldots$.. Self t's discounted utility from present and future consumption is:

$$u(c_t) + \beta \sum_{\tau=1}^{\infty} \delta^{\tau} u(c_{t+\tau}), \tag{2}$$

where$\beta$is assumed to be between zero and one. The parameter $\beta<1$ represents the "bias for the present."For $\beta=1$, these preferences are time-consistent. Laibson (1997) calls the discount structure in self t's lifetime utility "quasi-hyperbolic." An agent who discounts quasi-hyperbolically maximizes his / her intertemporal utility in expression (2). The quasi-hyperbolic discount function is a discrete time function with values $\{1, \beta\delta, \beta\delta^2, \beta\delta^3, \ldots\}$ (Phelps and Pollak, 1968). The discount factor between consecutive future periods (δ) is larger than between the current period and the next one ($\beta\delta$). Since $\beta$is taken to be less than one, a short-term discount factor is less than the long-term discount factor. In this functional form, the rate of substitution between today and tomorrow is smaller than that between any other pair of successive periods. Self t uses the lifetime utility function to evaluate the stream of payments from t onward. This implies that time inconsistency since δ (the marginal rate of substitution between t and $t+1$ from the point of view of any previous period) is replaced by $\beta\delta$ at t. The quasi-hyperbolic discount function is only "hyperbolic" in the sense that it captures the key qualitative property of the hyperbolic functions: a faster rate of decline in the short run than in the long run.Intertemporal tradeoffs shift with the mere passage of time, and plans or projects that seemed optimal yesterday need no longer be optimal today. In the original psychology research, hyperbolic discount functions are like $1/\tau$ and $1/(1+\alpha\tau)$with $\alpha> 0$, which generalize simpler hyperbolas.

The dynamic inconsistency forces the hyperbolic consumer to grapple with intrapersonal strategic conflict. Let us simply consider a three-period hyperbolic model, the shortest possible that actually generates time

---

[3] In Gul and Pesendorfer (2001), the agent's preferences do not change between periods (there is no dynamic inconsistency). They propose that "temptation" rather than a preference change may be the cause of a preference for commitment. Their dynamically consistent decision maker is unambiguously better off when ex ante undesirable temptations are no longer available.

inconsistency effect. The periods are labeled 0, 1, 2, and subscripts on c refer to the period in question. In period 0, self 0's discounted utility is:

$$u(c_0) + \beta\delta u(c_1) + \beta\delta^2 u(c_2), \quad (3)$$

while in period 1, self 1's discounted utility is:

$$u(c_1) + \beta\delta u(c_2). \quad (4)$$

For self 0, the discount factor between period 0 and period 1 is $\beta\delta$, and between period 1 and period 2 it is δ. Self 1's discount factor between period 1 and period 2 is $\beta\delta$. Therefore, there is a conflict between different selves about how much to consume in a given period. The consumer is dynamically inconsistent when β differs from one. When $\beta=1$, we are back to the case of a dynamically consistent consumer, with exponential discounting. This hyperbolic model captures a specific type of self-control problem. Since the discount factor self 0 applies between periods 1 and 2 (δ) is greater than the discount factor self 1 applies between the same two periods ($\beta\delta$), self 0 would like to behave more patiently in period 1 than self 1 actually does. Self 0 benefits from self-control that brings period-1 behavior in line with his / her wishes. Since each self consumes too much from earlier selves' point of view, each of them would agree to increase savings a little bit in exchange for later selves doing the same. All intertemporal selves could be made better off if all of them saved a little bit more. By making the implicit parameter restriction $\beta = 1$, standard economic models assume that no such self-control problem exists.

A single individual is modeled as many separate selves, one for each period. The future selves will control his / her future behavior. There is an important problem whether a person has beliefs about how his / her future selves will behave.

A "sophisticated" person exactly knows what his / her future selves' preferences will be. The sophisticated consumer chooses c_0 to maximize (3), knowing that in period 1 the consumption levels c_1 and c_2 will be chosen by self 1 with the discounted utility given by (4). Thus, self 0 takes actions that seek to constrain self 1. Sophisticates realize that they have hyperbolic preferences, and are fully aware of their future self-control problems. However, self 0 might expect self 1 to carry out the wishes of self 0.

Consumers might make current choices under the false beliefs that future selves will act in the interests of the current self.

A"naive" person believes that future selves' preferences will be identical to those of the current self. Naivesare fully unaware of their future self-control problems. The hyperbolic consumer may or may not be aware that his / her preferences will change over time. O'Donoghue and Rabin (1999a) make a comparison of these two extreme types.[4] Actual behavior is likely best described by something between naives and sophisticates, not just the two extremes. Self 0 may believe with certainty that the discount factor between periods 1 and 2 is $\beta^*\delta$.The parameter β^* reflects self 0's beliefs about his / her future β, so that $\beta^* = \beta$corresponds to sophisticates, and $\beta^* = 1$ corresponds tonaives.

Procrastination occurs when present costs are unduly salient in comparison with future costs, leading individuals to postpone tasks until tomorrow without foreseeing that when tomorrow comes, the required action will be delayed yet again (Akerlof, 1991). Akerlof (1991) implicitly corresponds to a model of time-inconsistent procrastination, highlighting the role of naive beliefs. Hyperbolic agents procrastinate because they think that whatever they will be doing later will not be as important as what they are doing now.O'Donoghue and Rabin (1999b) explore procrastination in terms of time-inconsistent preferences. Time-consistent agents do not procrastinate. Time-inconsistent agents, on the other hand, procrastinate.[5]

2.2. ADDICTION

It is often difficult to wait for a delayed reward when an immediately gratifying alternative is available. This is related to theories of addiction. Although people initially decide to take a far-sighted course of action (quitting smoking), they subsequently succumb to temptation. One element common to addictions is the addict's inability to escape when he / she wants to. The

---

[4] O'Donoghue and Rabin (2001) examine behavior for a person who is "partially naive." A partially naive person is aware that he / she has future self-control problem, but underestimates its magnitude.

[5] Fudenberg and Levine (2006) propose a "dual-self" model in which many sorts of decision problems can be viewed as a game between a sequence of short-run impulsive selves and a long-run patient self. In their model, the patient long-run self and a sequence of myopic short-run selves share the same preferences over stage-game outcomes. They differ only in how they regard the future.

immediacy of reward associated with smoking clearly has some importance in understanding why quitting can be difficult. The rewards from smoking are immediate and the adverse consequences tend to be delayed. People who become addicted may get greater (or longer) pleasure from their substances, and may also discount future rewards more sharply. Self-control can be defined as efforts made by the individual to avoid or resist behaving inconsistently.

Becker and Murphy (1988) study consumption of an addictive good in a standard exponential discounting model. Exponential discount functions predict consistency of preferences over time. A single utility function describes both the addict's and the non-addict's behavior. Rational addiction means that the addict's behavior, as well as the non-addict's behavior, maximizes utility in the long run according to some particular utility function. In Becker and Murphy (1988), people are aware of the addictive nature of cigarette smoking and they choose to smoke simply because the lifetime benefits are greater than the costs. Greater past consumption of addictive goods increases the desire for present consumption ("reinforcement"). The consumption of addictive goods at different times are complements. Consumption today increases the likelihood of consumption tomorrow, and the fear of addiction may generate conducts that resemble compulsive behavior.An increase in either past or expected future prices decreases current consumption. The price-theoretic framework yields the prediction that addicts will respond much more to permanent than to temporary price changes. Becker and Murphy (1988) show that the existence of multiple stable steady-state equilibria where agents either abstain or consume substantially.

Gruber and Köszegi (2001) incorporate time-inconsistent preferences into Becker and Murphy's (1988) rational addiction model. Forward-looking behavior does not imply time consistency. The purpose of Gruber and Köszegi (2001) is to show that a time-inconsistent model, where agents are forward-looking but have time-inconsistent preferences, can generate the Becker and Murphy's (1988) prediction that current consumption depends positively on future consumption. An implication of time-inconsistent preferences is that individuals, who realize their self-control problems, have a demand for commitment devices.

Let a_t and c_t denote the consumption of the addictive and the "ordinary" (non-addictive) goods in period t, respectively. Furthermore, let S_t denote the period t stock of past consumption (the stock of "addictive capital"). $S_t$depends on past consumption of a and on life cycle events, and it evolves as follows:

$$S_{t+1} = (1-\eta)(S_t + a_t),$$

where η is the depreciation rate of the stock. Instantaneous utility is additively separable in these two goods:

$$U_t = U(a_t, c_t, S_t) = v(a_t, S_t) + u(c_t).$$

There are two extreme kinds of hyperbolic discounters: naives and sophisticates. This can be modeled as a sequential game played by the successive intertemporal selves. For a naive agent, self t does not realize that self t+1 will in turn overvalue period t+1. A naive agent maximizes (2), unconscious of the fact that his / her future selves will change the plans. On the other hand, for a sophisticated agent, self t knows that self t+1 will want to do something other than what self t would have him / her do. Sophisticated agents have a demand for self-control devices if they want to quit.[6]

In the context of hyperbolic discounting, players are not separate individuals, but they are different intertemporal incarnations of the same individual. This form of discounting sets up a conflict between the preferences of different intertemporal selves. The agent's long-run preferences are taken as those relevant for social welfare maximization. In the standard rational addiction model, the optimal tax on addictive goods should depend only on the externalities that their use imposes on society. Sophisticates try to influence the future selves through their current consumption of addictive goods. They feel a need to exert control on the future selves by consuming less. This effect helps the government. Smokers who have an intention to quit smoking will support for anti-smoking public policies. In the time-inconsistent alternative model, optimal government policy should depend also on the "internalities" that consumers impose on themselves. Due to the existence of "internality," there is a room for government intervention, e.g., a tax hike could be welfare improving.

We can think about price interventions of the following form. The hyperbolic consumer lives for three periods, t = 0, 1, 2. Consumption only occurs in period 1.An adjustment is added to the per-unit price that the consumer faces in period 1. In that period, the consumer has to make a choice

[6] A recent line of research has shown how the combination of self-control and informational concerns can account for forms of "motivated cognitions" documented by psychologists. For example, in Bénabou and Tirole (2004), a person may achieve self-control through the adoption of personal rules based on self-reputation over one's willpower.

between goods a and c. Good a may be pleasant to consume in period 1, but it causes harm in period 2. Consumption of one unit of good a leads to harm $h>0$ in period 2. Good c is an ordinary good that is pleasant to consume at the moment and that has no implications for future utility. Normalize the price of good c in period 1 to 1.

We consider the per-period utility functions as follows:

$$u_t = \begin{cases} 0 & \text{in period } t = 0 \\ v(a) + c & \text{in period } t = 1 \\ -ha & \text{in period } t = 2 \end{cases}$$

Self 0′s discounted utility function is:

$$u_0 + \beta\delta u_1 + \beta\delta^2 u_2,$$

while self 1′s discounted utility function is:

$$u_1 + \beta\delta u_2.$$

The parameters β and δ are between 0 and 1. Then self 0 would like self 1 to discount period 2 relative to period 1 by a factor of δ. Hence self 0 prefers that self 1 counts the future implications of consuming each unit of good a at a value of δh. However, self 1's discount factor between period 1 and period 2 is βδ.Self 1 only counts the future implications of consuming a at a value of $\beta\delta h$. To align self 1′s interests with those of self 0, we can impose a price adjustment of $\delta h - \beta\delta h = (1-\beta)\,\delta h$ per unit of good a. Due to this change in price, self 1 is forced to fully internalize the future harm of consumption.

In hyperbolic models, a person discounts heavily between the present and all future periods, but does not discount so heavily between future periods. Following Kan (2007), let us consider a simple model of decision making by an infinitely lived smoker. In the model an infinitely lived smoker faces two choices: to continue smoking or to quit. The two choices yield different paths of lifetime utilities:

{S, S, S, ...}, if a smoker continues smoking,

and

{Q, N, N, ...}, if a smoker quits smoking,

where S, Q, and N are per-period utility, with Q < S < N. The utility in the period when a smoker quits, Q, is assumed to be less than that if he / she smokes in that period, S (the disutility from quitting). S < N is due to the fact that smoking is harmful.

A smoker quits in the current period if:

$$Q+\beta\sum_{t=1}^{\infty}\delta^{t}N > S+\beta\sum_{t=1}^{\infty}\delta^{t}S,$$

$$S-Q < \frac{\beta\delta}{1-\delta}(N-S).$$

Thus, the cost of quitting is smaller than the lifetime gain from not smoking.

Instead of quitting in the current period, a smoker may consider quitting in the next period. From the perspective of the current period, he / she plans to quit in the next period if:

$$\beta Q+\beta\sum_{t=1}^{\infty}\delta^{t}N > \beta S+\beta\sum_{t=1}^{\infty}\delta^{t}S,$$

$$S-Q < \frac{\delta}{1-\delta}(N-S).$$

Since $\beta \leq 1$, a smoker is more likely to plan to quit in the next period than to actually quit in the current period.

If the following inequality holds, the individual is a perpetual procrastinator.

$$\frac{\beta\delta}{1-\delta}(N-S) < S-Q < \frac{\delta}{1-\delta}(N-S). \tag{5}$$

When (5) holds, a smoker will not quit in the current period, but will plan to quit in the next period. However, when the next period arrives, the smoker will again postpone the plan to quit for one more period. This postponing will continue forever.

2.3. RETIREMENT

Actual retirement savings decisions are complicated by behavioral factors that may interfere with the ability of agents to make and execute plans in accord with the conventional economic theory. According to the well-known life-cycle hypothesis, people want to have a stable consumption across all periods in their remaining lifetime. Then people rationally determine how much they can consume over the remainder of their life by taking their assets and all future earnings into account. Furthermore, in any given year, the difference between the level of consumption and income will be the amount saved (or borrowed). The young borrow to pay for consumption, the middle-aged save for retirement, and the old spend those savings.

People may decide how much to save in a variety of ways that are susceptible to behavioral factors. Although people have preferences for saving in order to have a smooth consumption stream, they also have preferences for immediate gratification. Time inconsistent consumers may formulate the same future saving plan as a conventional life-cycle planner, but engage in short-term behavior that violates the plan. Sophisticates can overcome this problem by engaging in commitment mechanisms that restrict future actions.

Diamond and Köszegi (2003) incorporate time-inconsistent preferences into the analysis of endogenous retirement decisions. An agent who discounts quasi-hyperbolically maximizes his / her intertemporal utility in expression (2). For self t, the discount factor between periods t and $t+1$ is$\beta\delta$, and between any two adjacent periods later it is δ.There is a single period in which the agent can choose whether to work or retire.

Following Diamond and Köszegi (2003), let us consider a three-period hyperbolic model, the shortest possible that actually generates time inconsistency effect. The periods are labeled 0, 1, 2, and subscripts on c and W refer to the period in question. In period 0, the agent has to work. In period 1, the agent can decide whether to work or retire, and in period 2, he / she has to be retired. The agent incurs an additive constant utility cost of effort, $e > 0$, if he / she works in period 1. The agent also gets an extra amount of income, $\Delta > 0$, if he / she works in period 1.

The middle period is the retirement decision period, period 1. Suppose that, at the beginning of period 1, self 1 inherits a wealth of W_1. If self 1 works, he / she will have $W_1 + \Delta$.If self 1 retires, W_1 will be the remaining wealth. It is assumed that self 1 will consume a proportion γ (> 0) of the wealth W_1. Furthermore, let R denote the exogenous gross return on wealth.

If self 1 retires, the discounted utility is:

$$u(\gamma W_1) + \beta\delta u(R(1-\gamma)W_1).$$

If self 1 works, the discounted utility is:

$$u(\gamma(W_1 + \Delta)) + \beta\delta u(R(1-\gamma)(W_1 + \Delta)) - e.$$

Therefore, self 1 will work if and only if:

$$u(\gamma(W_1 + \Delta)) - u(\gamma W_1) + \beta\delta u(R(1-\gamma)(W_1 + \Delta)) - \beta\delta u(R(1-\gamma)W_1) \geq e. \quad (6)$$

From the point of view of self 0, he / she will prefer self 1to work if:

$$\beta\delta u(\gamma(W_1 + \Delta)) - \beta\delta u(\gamma W_1) + \beta\delta^2 u(R(1-\gamma)(W_1 + \Delta)) - \beta\delta^2 u(R(1-\gamma)W_1) \geq \beta\delta e.$$

or

$$u(\gamma(W_1 + \Delta)) - u(\gamma W_1) + \delta u(R(1-\gamma)(W_1 + \Delta)) - \delta u(R(1-\gamma)W_1) \geq e. (7)$$

The left-hand side of (7) is greater than the left-hand side of (6). Therefore, there is a range of wealth levels for which self 1would retire, but self 0 would like self 1 to work. In a quasi-hyperbolic framework, there will be circumstances in which self0 would want self 1 to work (for the benefit of self 2), but self 1 does not want to work. In order to avoid this outcome, self 0 might save less to force self 1 to work. On the other hand, if self 0 would like self 1 to work, but it is too expensive to achieve this without commitment, self 0 will save more to help finance self 1's unavoidable retirement.

Chapter 3

IDENTITY

3.1. IDENTITY IN UTILITY

At a very basic level, most people are aware of how they are differentiated from their surroundings. People often receive themselves as members of social groups. Such group memberships may affect behavior in ways that cannot easily be reduced to material self-interest. This notion is commonly referred to as an individual's sense of self. Akerlof and Kranton (2000) introduce "identity," a person's sense of self, into a standard utility function framework. They use the utility function simply as a description of motivation.Each person has a conception of his / her own social categories and that of other people. Identity further depends on the extent to which one's own given characteristics match the ideal of one's assigned category. In other words, identity is associated with the social environment and expected respective behavior (a prescription or norm for behavior).

For each person *j*, identity, or self-image, is treated as an argument in the utility function:

$$U_j = U_j(\mathbf{a}_j, \mathbf{a}_{-j}, I_j).$$

Here, utility depends on*j*'s identity, or self-imageI_j, and also on the vectors of *j*'s actions $\mathbf{a}_j$ and others' actions$\mathbf{a}_{-j}$.

A person *j*'s identity, or self-image itself, is represented as:

$$I_j = I_j(\mathbf{a}_j, \mathbf{a}_{-j}, \mathbf{c}_j, \varepsilon_j, \mathbf{P}).$$

A person j's identity I_j depends on j's actions and the actions of others, on j's assigned social categories $\mathbf{c}_j$, on j's own given characteristicsε_j, and on· the extent to which$\varepsilon_j$match the ideal of j's assigned category, indicated by the prescription **P**.

A person's sense of self is associated with different social categories and how people in these categories should behave. Examples of social categories include racial and ethnic designations. Akerlof and Kranton's(2000) model shows that individuals have an incentive to choose particular actions such that their own individual characteristics fit with the socially determined self-image of the social categories to which they belong. The utility function is an expression that characterizes what a person cares about. In their model,U_j depends on I_j. This serves to pick out each separate individual. Deviations from the prescription then generate disutility.

In their prototype model, identity depends on two social categories, Green and Red, and the correspondence of own and others' actions to behavioral prescriptions for their category. There are two possible activities, Activity One and Activity Two. Each person has a taste for either Activity. They consider an interaction between an individual with a taste for Activity One (Person One) and an individual with a taste for Activity Two (Person Two). If Person One (or Two) undertakes Activity One (or Two), he / she earns some positive utility. A person who chooses the activity that does not match his / her taste earns zero utility. As behavioral prescriptions, Greens should engage in Activity One, and Reds should engage in Activity Two. For example, by choosing Activity One, a person could affirm his / her identity as a Green. First, identity changes the payoffs from one's own actions. Person One who chooses Activity Two would lose his / her Green identity. Second, identity changes the payoffs of others' actions (externality). If Person One and Person Two are paired, Activity Two on the part of Person Twodiminishes Person One's Green identity. Third, the choice of different identities affect an individual's economic behavior. While Person Two could choose between Green or Red, he / she could never be a "true" Green. Finally, the social categories and behavioral prescriptions can be changed, affecting identity-based preferences.

Akerlof and Kranton (2002) construct a model of a student's utility where identity is salient. In a standard model of education, a student's utility will depend on his / her effort in school and the pecuniary returns to this effort. Let $e_i$be individual i's effort in school. The pecuniary benefits of e_i are the returns to skills in the labor market, $wk(e_i)$, where w is the wage rate per unit of skill and$k(e_i)$ is i's skills (or human capital). Akerlof and Kranton (2002) add identity to student i's utility function. In the school context, for example, social identities may include "jocks" or "nerds." Students also have ideas about how people in groups should behave. Prescriptions **P** give the ideal characteristics and behavior for each category. A student thinks of oneself and others according to different categories. Student i is assigned to a social categoryc_i and one's own characteristics ε_j.Student i's identity, I_i, depends on the match between his / her characteristics and behavior with the ideal for his / her category. Then, student i's utility is:

$$U_i = U_i(wk(e_i), e_i, I_i),$$

where

$$I_i = I_i(e_i, c_i; \varepsilon_j, \mathbf{P}).$$

Gains and losses in identity are the gains and losses in utility derived from the term I_i.

Furthermore, Akerlof and Kranton (2005) construct a model of identity in organizations. The model depicts the interaction between a firm and a worker. The worker can take on an identity as part of the organization. The firm and the worker face the following production technology. The worker can take only two actions: a high-effort action, A, and a low-effort action, B. The high-effort action increases the likelihood that the firm's revenues will take on a high value rather than a low value. Though the firm cannot observe the effort of the worker, it can observe whether revenues are high or low. To give the worker the incentive to take the high-effort action A, the firm will pay a high wage when it observes high revenues and a low wage when it observes low revenues. With a sufficiently large difference in these wages, the worker will take the high-effort action A. In their model, the worker can take on two different identities: an insider, N, and an outsider, O. In one case, the worker identifies with the worker (an insider N). The norm for an insider is to act in the interest of the firm and to do the high-effort action A. When a worker has this identity, he / she loses some utility insofar as he / she deviates from the ideal action of A. On the other hand, the worker may not identify with the firm (an outsider O). The norm for an outsider is to do the least possible effort on the job (or to do the low-effort action B). The worker will lose some utility insofar as he / she deviates from the low-effort ideal of B. In the formula, the worker can take on only two categories, $c = N$ or O. The overall utility of the worker, U, is then summarized by:

$$U(y,e;c)=\ln y-e+I_c-t_c\,|\,e^*(c)-e\,|,$$

where y is the worker's income, e is his / her actual effort, c is his / her social category, I_c is his / her identity utility from being in category c, and the last term represents the disutility from diverging the ideal effort level for category c, denoted by$e^*(c)$. In the formula, the worker's utility varies with his / her category c as either an insider N or an outsider O. Furthermore, the worker's utility depends on the deviation of one's own effort from the ideal for one's respective social category, according to one's identity and situation. The formula thus captures the notion of norms and ideals.

3.2. Culture

What is the substance of culture? Culture is complex and it ranges from underlying beliefs and assumptions to visible structures and practices. The study of culture has been overwhelmingly the province of anthropology. For example, in Harris (1975), "a culture is the total socially acquired life-way or life-style of a group of people. It consists of the patterned, repetitive ways of thinking, feeling, and acting that are characteristic of the members of a particular society or segment of a society."Numerous cross-cultural studies have demonstrated how peoples'life-styles are influenced by cultural factors. As an example, individualism/collectivism describes the relationship between the individual and the prevailing collectivity in society. Individualism implies a loose social framework in which people focus on their goals, needs, and rights more than community concerns. On the other hand, collectivism is characterized by a tight social framework in which people value in-group goals and concerns.

Culture is taken to be what social influence influences (Axelrod, 1997). In fact, humans acquire large parts of their behavioral repertoire via forms of social learning (basically imitation). Understanding how people learn from others is important not only for understanding individual decisions, but also for comprehending patterns of change and variation among human groups. Every group has its own distinctive culture, but the cultures of groups can be more similar because individuals in one group learn some of their beliefs, behavioral norms, and values from individuals in the other group with which they interact.However, differences among individuals can exist because they acquire different behaviors as a result of some form of social learning. In

Axelrod's (1997) model, two groups that are already culturally similar are more likely to interact and, therefore, to be even more culturally similar. On the contrary, two neighboring groups with zero cultural similarity are unlikely to interact and, therefore, will have no tendency to be more culturally similar.

Culture affects individuals' values. Values are incorporated into individual preference functions through the sociological mechanism known as "socialization" and the psychological mechanism known as "internalization of norms" (Gintis, 2003).[1] Culture can be largely defined in terms of the cognitive content and processes that are common to a group of people. It is the result of social interaction and is shared. A cultural group consists of individuals who share a set of beliefs that is recognizably different from those of other groups. Cultural factors can be an additional variable in the production function (Altman, 2001). Cultural norms that result in a less than full work ethic create x-inefficiency. Standard economic theory does not allow for this because it assumes that, in any economic context, all agents will be obliged by competition to become utility maximizers.

Teraji (2008) investigates how culture affects economic outcomes in a behavioral model of the firm hierarchy, which consists of a principal and an agent. Differently from Akerlof and Kranton (2000), it introduces effort variability into the firm hierarchy model with different cultures and shows the co-existence of both efficient and inefficient equilibrium solutions. Standard economic models are based on the methodological individualism that postulates that preferences are strictly personal. Economists do not deny the need to inquire about preferences, but culture has not been seen as a problem for them. However, in real life, cultural aspects matter to most people. Preferences are not simply formed in isolation but are affected and shaped by the social categories to which individuals belong.

Defining culture as some notion of shared beliefs, expectations, customs, jargon, and rituals, Lazear (1999) investigates the role of language and cultural assimilation. If there are more than one culture in a country, a common culture facilitates trade between individuals, allowing them to have common expectations and customs. Members of a minority group may find it urgent to

---

[1] See Teraji (2007) for the process by which norms evolve exhibits generalized increasing returns. In a world of increasing returns to scale ("positive feedbacks"), initial and trivial circumstances can have important and irreversible influences on the ultimate market allocation of resources. Path-dependent economics is a theory of equilibrium selection with positive feedbacks, and path-dependent outcome is associated with characteristics of persistence and uniformity. The economy has a multiplicity of possible equilibrium solutions, where the dominant solution can be the sub-optimal one.

coordinate with the majority of the society. Minority members may be assimilated in order to survive in the society.

Culture relates to core organizational values. All organizations have cultures that influence the way people behave in a variety of areas such as the rites, rituals, routines, and the language used. Organizations tend to be effective if they have cultures that are well coordinated. However, the cross-cultural interactions bring together people who may have different patterns of behaving and believing. Changing from one's own culture to the alternative organizational culture can be uncomfortable. Focusing on costly cultural assimilation in organizations, Teraji (2008) studies culture as a determinant of different economic outcomes among firms.

Teraji (2008) considers a simple hierarchy composed of a principal (she) and an agent (he). A principal and an agent are matched in pairs. Let π be the (pecuniary) total benefit when the project is implemented. Individual interactions are not governed by complete enforceable contracts. Effort is not subject to contract. Although no enforceable contract can be signed ex ante, the two parties bargain over the benefitπ. Let $(1-\alpha)\pi$, where $0 < \alpha < 1$, denote the principal's benefit when the project is implemented. Similarly, $\alpha\pi$ is the agent's benefit when the project is implemented.Teraji (2008) supposes that there exist two cultures in society, culture A and culture B. Furthermore, principals are assumed to belong to culture A. On the other hand, each agent may belong to one of two cultures. Thus, one principal may match with an agent from culture B.

The principal's effort translates a blueprint with probability$E$ and into no blueprint with probability $1-E$. Let e_B denote effort exerted by the agent from culture B. Then the agent from culture B implements the blueprint with probability e_B and does not implement it with $1-e_B$. All blueprints are assumed to yield the same benefit. In the model, economic outcomes are distinguished only by the amounts of effort supplied by each party.

Thus, $e_B E(1-\alpha)\pi$ is the principal's ex ante expected benefit if she hires the agent from culture B. On the other hand, $e_B E\alpha\pi$ is the agent's ex ante expected benefit if he belongs to culture B originally. The principal chooses how much effort to devote to developing the blueprint. Developing the blueprint generates some private cost$g(E)$ for the principal. More specifically, this is assumed to generate some convex cost, i.e., $g(E) = (1/2)E^2$. Therefore, the more the principal exerts effort, the higher is the marginal cost of further effort. Furthermore, to make the analysis tractable, each agent picks his own effort in some interval $[0, \hat{e}]$, where $0 < \hat{e} \leq 1$, and that he has linear disutility of effort in this interval. This interval $[0, \hat{e}]$ is constant for each agent. For example, the time spent on the project is limited in a day. The common maximum effort is assumed to be $\hat{e}$. On the other hand, if the agent does not implement the project, his effort level is 0 (the common minimum effort). Then he receives no benefit. Thus, the agent from culture B implements the blueprint with probabilitye_B by exerting some cost $\gamma_B e_B$ in the interval $[0, \hat{e}]$, where $\gamma_B > 0$.

Each firm requires an agent to coordinate on the principal's culture, i.e., culture A. All agents must adopt culture A to work. However, changing cultures is more costly if the agent belongs to culture B by nature. Coordination on the principal's culture thus requires an additional cost for the agent from culture B. The parameter γ_B is supposed to contain such an additional cost when he exerts effort in the firm hierarchy. It is costly for the agent to adopt the alternative culture in the work environment.

If a principal matches with an agent from culture B, the two parties' expected relevant utilities are given by:

$$U = e_B E(1-\alpha)\pi - (1/2)E^2$$

and

$$u_B = e_B E\alpha\pi - \gamma_B e_B.$$

The first order conditions of the two parties with respect to these effort levels E and e_B are:

Principal: $E = e_B(1-\alpha)\pi$

and

$$e_B = \hat{e} \text{ if } E\alpha\pi \geq \gamma_B$$

Agent:

$$e_B = 0 \quad \text{if } E\alpha\pi < \gamma_B.$$

Therefore, we can compute the Nash equilibrium effort levels, (e_B^*, E^*), in the firm hierarchy.

$$e_B^* = \hat{e} \text{ and } E^* = \hat{e}(1-\alpha)\pi \quad \text{if } k \geq \gamma_B,$$

and

$$e_B^* = 0 \text{ and } E^* = 0 \qquad \text{if } k<\gamma_B$$

where

$$k \equiv \hat{e}(1-\alpha)\,\alpha\pi^2.$$

Thus, if $\gamma_B$is so large that $k<\gamma_B$ holds, the agent from culture B supplies the minimum level of effort 0 and the principal supplies the effort level 0 as a result. Culture is a kind of meta-preference. If cultural assimilation occurs, it is costly for the agent from culture B to coordinate on culture A. In the utility function, cultural differences reflectγ_B. If the agent's disutility to change from culture B to culture A is sufficiently large, he supplies the minimum level of effort, that is, $e_B = 0$. On the other hand, if the disutility for the agent of culture B is sufficiently small, he supplies the maximum level of effort, that is, $e_B = \hat{e}$ (>0). If cultural differences exist, effort inputs can vary. Given effort variability, effort complementarities between the principal's effort and the agent's effort allow for the sub-optimal equilibrium solution in the firm hierarchy. Changing cultures can generate inefficient economic environments if effort is a discretionary variable.

Preferences are not simply formed in isolation."Preferences are learned as an accent or a taste for a national cuisine is acquired, that is, by processes which may but need not be intentional" (Bowles, 1998). Culture is the non-market factor. Culture is, was, and will be a major characteristic of the human being. Market forces cannot deprive the agent of his cultural identity. Even though the agent knows that his original culture causes the inefficient outcome, he hesitates to abandon it. Therefore, organizations are expected to manage cultural diversity effectively. In order to avoid the negative consequences of cultural assimilation, some adaptations must be achieved through a long-term process. When different cultural groups are in contact over a long period of time, they are involved in a process of various changes, denoted as the "acculturation" process. Acculturation is a process of changes that involve various forms of mutual accommodation, leading to some long-term psychological and socio-cultural adaptations between both cultures. Acculturation is distinguished from assimilation. Acculturation takes place in the dominant group as well as in the non-dominant group. The dominant group's acculturation orientations indicate whether the dominant group allows the non-dominant group members to maintain their own culture. When both groups prefer similar acculturation orientations, the long-term relationship between the groups will be consensual. Then the agent will not suffer a utility (or virtue) loss for the self-inflicted loss of cultural identity in the long run. Cultural sensitivity is thus needed. People have to be aware well of cultural differences, know why differences exist, and accommodate these differences within organizations.

Cognition includes the process used to predict what others are going to do. People are likely to perceive bits of information that is germane to existing schemata knowledge structures that represent objects or events and provide default assumptions about their characteristics, relationships, and entailments under conditions of incomplete information (DiMaggio, 1997). Agents experience culture as schematic structures that organize that information.Culture represents the set of living styles and traditions, shared by the members of a group. Individuals with common cultural backgrounds will share cognitive systems inter-subjectively. Henrich (2004) proposes culture as the mechanism reducing intra-group differences and maintaining inter-group differences, by biasing individuals in favor of copying the common ideas, beliefs, and values. Patterns of culture may vary widely in human societies based on the different kinds of cultural transmission. Culturally transmitted ideas, beliefs, and values are important for understanding human behavior. As Henrich (2004) suggests, cultural evolution is likely to proceed much more rapidly than genetic evolution because cultural transmission can spread novel behaviors, ideas, and practices among populations within a single generation. Furthermore, cultural transmission is likely to be more subject to drift and random variation than genetic transmission. Human groups under cultural evolution will drift into the domains of attraction of alternative equilibria more often than in genetic evolution.

In the ultimatum bargaining game, the first player (the "proposer") proposes a division of a fixed amount of money that may be accepted or rejected by the second player (the "responder"). If the responder accepts the proposed division of the sum of money (the "pie"), then the division is as proposed by the proposer. If the responder rejects the proposed division, each player earns nothing. Then, the subgame perfect equilibrium gives all the bargaining power to the proposer. That is, any demand that leaves the second player with anything should be accepted, and consequently the proposer should get almost all of the pie. In contrast, results from ultimatum game experiments show that proposers do not demand nearly this amount, generally demanding between 50 % and 60 % of the total.

The experiment in Roth, Prasnikar, Okuno-Fujiwara, Zamir (1991) is the first cross-country comparison study on ultimatum bargaining in the United States, Israel, Japan, and Slovenia. In this experiment, subjects were first assigned a role: proposers or responders. They played the game in their respective roles for 10 rounds, each time with a different, anonymous, and randomly selected opponent. The pie was worth the equivalent of $10 in terms of purchasing power in all four countries. Subjects were paid according to their monetary payoffs in one randomly selected round. The responder can accept or reject the offer. If the responder accepts the offer, the proposer gets the demanded amount and the responder gets the remainder. If the responder rejects, neither player receives anything.

Roth et al.'s (1991) experimental results can be summarized as follows:

- The frequencies of the offers implied by the subgame perfect equilibrium of the game ranged from 1% of the time in Slovenia to 9.3% in Israel.
- Offers were highest in the United States and Slovenia, then in Japan, and lowest in Israel.
- The conditional frequency of rejected offers is inversely related to the fraction of the pie offered. That is, low offers are rejected more frequently than high offers. The conditional frequencies of acceptance of offers were lowest in Slovenia, then in the United States, and highest in Israel and Japan.
- Furthermore, the probability that a given offer is rejected is lower in countries where lower offers were observed.

Thus, Roth et al. (1991) find "small,"significant differences in the ultimatum game. They conclude that these differences can be explained as "cultural differences."Camerer (2003) argues that cross-cultural comparison raises at least four difficult methodological problems: stakes, languages, experimenter interactions, and confounds. (1) Controlling for stakes requires the experimenter to match the purchasing power of the stake in different cultures. (2) Keeping the meaning of instructions as constant as possible is important. (3) The biggest mistake in controlling for identity is to use a different experimenter in each culture. The ideal experimenters speak both languages and are perceived similarly in both cultures. (4) It is extremely difficult to avoid the effects of potentially important variables that are confounded with culture (causing "identification problems" in econometrics terms).

In the ultimatumgame, existing experimental data and analyses have shown that subjects from industrial societies behave almost similarly; the mean offer from proposers averages between 40 % and 50% of the total, and responders often reject offers lower than 20% of the total. However, Henrich (2000) shows that the Machiguengaof the Peruvian Amazon behave very differently from subjects drawn from industrial societies in the ultimatum game. For the Machiguenga, the economic unit is the family; families fully produce for their own needs (food, clothing, etc.) and do not rely on institutions or other families for their social or economic welfare. Cooperation above the family level is almost unknown, and the Machiguenga are quite socially disconnected. In Henrich's (2000) test, Machiguenga proposers offered only 26% of the total sum, and responders almost always accept offers less than 20% of the total. Machiguenga proposers seem to possess little or no sense of obligation to provide an equal share to responders, and responders seem to have little or no expectation of receiving an equal share. Cultural differences greatly influence economic behavior.

Henrich, Boyd, Bowles, Camerer, Fehr, Gintis, and McElreach (2001) recruited subjects from 15 small-scale societies to expand the diversity of economic and cultural conditions in various games including the ultimatum game. Their sample consist of three foraging groups, six slash-and-burn horticulturists, four nomadic herding groups, and two sedentary, small-scale agricultural societies. Henrich et al.'s (2001) experimental results can be summarized as follows:

- The canonical model of self-interested behavior is not supported in any society studied.
- There is considerably more behavioral variability across groups than had been found in previous cross-cultural research. The mean offers from proposers ranged from 26% to 58%. The most common behavior for the Machiguenga was to offer zero. In some groups, rejections were extremely rare, even in the presence of very low offers, while, in others, rejection rates were substantial, including frequent rejections of offers above 50%.
- Group-level differences in economic organization and the degree of market integration explain a substantial portion of the behavioral variation across societies; the higher the degree of market integration and the higher the payoffs to cooperation, the greater the level of cooperation and sharing in experimental games.

- Individual-level economic and demographic variables do not explain behavior either within or across groups.
- Behavior in the experiments is generally consistent with economic patterns of everyday life in these societies.

Why would people reject a positive amount of money? The responder would reject the offer because he / she is angry as being treated unfairly, and he / she is willing to pay to hurt the person who perpetrated this unfairness. This is not just a matter of developing a capability for anger, but rather a matter for developing a cognitive understanding of whether an angry response is appropriate. What matters is that the "right" response is elicited in the "right" settings. Pro-social emotions (the empathy people feel towards those who have been kind to them and the hostility towards those who have not)thus serve to enhance the individual and group fitness in the social conditions. This reflects strong reciprocity, namely a propensity to reward those who have behaved cooperatively and correspondingly to punish those who have violated norms of acceptable behavior, even when reward and punishment cannot be justified in terms of outcome-oriented preferences.

Trust is based on a cognitive process. Individuals cognitively choose whether they trust others or not. People attempt to createmental models, or internal representations, in order to interpret the environment. Ideologies are the shared framework of mental models that groups of individuals possess. As Denzau and North (1994) point out, individuals with common cultural backgrounds and experiences will share reasonably convergent mental models, ideologies, and institutions. Culture, as a system of beliefs and ideologies, provides shared collective understandings in shaping individuals' strategies. Culture is a possible determinant of economic performance. Cognition may have more subjective aspects, while culture enables individuals to develop inter-subjectively shared mental models. Culture affects belief systems about trust. The establishment of trust in interpersonal relations depends on shared mental models. Different cultures may imply different ways in which agents apply a specific logic of action. Economic performance can be explained on the basis of different belief systems. Trust arises from the cultural component which affects individual belief systems.

Trust can be conceptualized as an inter-subjective or systematic social reality. Trust exists in a social system insofar as the members of that system act according to the presence of each other. Each person trusts on the expectation that others trust. Trust may decline in contexts of an increase of unknown outsiders. Individuals can develop trust because of the quality of the social system. Investments on community associations increase perceptions of security. Social capital generates positive externalities that are achieved through shared trust.

Furthermore, mental models and institutions are closely related. "Belief systems embody the internal representation of the human landscape. Institutions are the structure that humans impose on that landscape in order to produce the desired outcome. Beliefs systems therefore are the internal representation and institutions the external manifestation of that representation" (North, 2005, p.49). There is no understanding a social structure independently of the mental models or belief systems that help constitute that structure.

The behavioral economic model assumes that the quantity and quality of effort is a discretionary variable. Systems of shared mental models can produce "bad" institutions, in which sub-optimal economic performance can emerge. In order to foster economic progress, it is necessary to alter mental models that shape the way individuals think about trust. Economic performance can improve with trust. To trust others is one of the elements of a value system that favors economic prosperity. Shared trust confers social capital benefits for individuals by protecting property rights, reducing uncertainty and transaction costs, and building better bridges to economic opportunities. In contrast, mistrust is typical of communities that resist prosperity.

Chapter 4

POSSIBLE SELVES

Typically, the standard economic agents do not care about"who they are." In standard economic theory, the individual has a stable and consistent preference ordering over goods and actions. However, preferences are changing at the normal level of personality development. In psychology, people are likely to learn things about themselves and struggle with their identity. The self-concept is an individual's belief about his / her personal qualities and abilities. Our self-concept or identity has profound effects on the way we behave.Economists have largely neglected the self as a primary force of individual behavior.

Akerlof and Kranton (2000) emphasize the importance of identity, a person's sense of self, for economic decision making. They treat identity as an argument in a person's utility function. Identity in theutility function is based on social categories to which an individual belongs. Each individual possesses one particular collection of social characteristics. However, identity choice is very often limited in their framework.

The definitional unity of the self is called into serious question by the empirical inconsistencies of economic choice, and by the need to construct multiple-self theories to explain them (Lea and Webley, 2005). As Moldoveanu and Stevenson (2001) suggest, there are two models of the self: the self as a unified system and the self as fragmented entity. A multiplicity of selves is composed of a wide variety of unrelated and conflicting roles. People with multiple selves may make more rational and more adaptive decisions in economic affairs than people with a single unified self in some situations (Lester, 2003).[1]

People have an array of possible selves. Possible selves are representations of the self in the future and supply direction for the achievement of the desired goal. Possible selves are constituents of a differentiated, dynamic self-system. A given possible self might rarely be activated and, therefore, have little impact on current self-representation and behavior. Alternatively, that possible self might be activated and highly consequential for current representations of the self. Self-discrepancy theory (Higgins, 1987) indicates that a person possesses distinct domains of the self. The "actual" self refers to a representation of the attributes that we believe we currently possess. The"ideal" self refers to a representation of the attributes that we wish or hope to possess.[2]Internal change encompasses the production of possible selves. Possible selves are future-oriented schemata of what people believe they could potentially become. The self-system is multifaceted and dynamic, with different self-representations activated at different times. Possible selves serve as cognitive resources that motivate the self throughout personal development.

Comparison between the actual self and the ideal self has important motivational consequences. The actual-ideal congruency represents the presence of positive outcomes while the actual-ideal discrepancy represents the absence of these outcomes. The response to perceived discrepancy can be shaped toward desired behavioral change. Significant improvement may occur for individuals with plausibly self-regulatory possible selves. Self-regulation occurs with respect to the ideal self-guide. This reflects the desire to bring oneself closer to what one would ideally like to become. Actual-ideal self-regulation involves a promotion focus, that is, a concern with advancement, growth, and accomplishment.

Self-motives are mechanisms by which people create or maintain certain self-images in their own minds. Specifically, self-evaluation needs may be satisfied either through the positive enhancement of self-relevant information ("self-enhancement") or the affirmation of already existing self-conceptions ("self-verification"). Self-enhancement is the motivation to elevate positive

[1] As Pecchenino (2009) suggests, a person struggles to discover why and to become who he / she is, balancing and integrating many identities.

[2] Furthermore, the "ought"self refers to a representation of the attributes that we believe we should possess. Ought self-guides are associated with prevention goals that we strive to avoid. Discrepancies between the actual self and the ought self produce agitation-related emotions (anxiety, fear, or uneasiness).

aspects of one's self-concept or protect oneself from negative information. Self-enhancement has been identified as underlying people's tendency to believe that they have improved relative to the past and that their personal improvement has been greater than other people's (Leary, 1995). Self-enhancers are those individuals who perceive themselves more positively than they perceive others. However, self-verification is also an important factor in the individual's motivational system. Individuals desire not merely to know how great they are (self-enhancement), but also to confirm that they are the type they already thought they were (self-verification). Hence, persons might prefer to maintain a coherent image of who they are. Self-verification is defined as the desire to confirm pre-existing self-views (subjectively accurate). According to self-verification theory, a preference for self-verifying evaluations should emerge even though the self-view happens to be negative. Self-verifying information leads to stability in people's self-concepts and makes people feel that they understand themselves (Swann et al., 1992). Self-verification involves the impulse to act in accordance with the pre-existing self-concept and to maintain it intact in the face of any discordant piece of information about it.

Affective components gradually receive a growing amount of attention.[3] Motives and emotions are strongly linked. Most judgments and most choices are made intuitively (Kahneman, 2003).[4] People experience self-conscious emotions when they become aware that they have lived up to, or failed to live up to, some actual or ideal self-representation. An actual-ideal discrepancy might result in depression, disappointment, or sadness (dejection-related emotions).

Teraji (2009) proposes an economic model of how intentional self-change occurs.The model presents a mechanism for intentional self-change over time. Intentional self-change is an effort to construct a particular kind of self. There is no reason to suppose that individuals always remain the same. Intentional self-change redefines who one is.The model provides a simple theory of the decision to change oneself, considering the capacity of the self for change. This change will motivate individuals to revise their ideas and develop different characteristics. Then, their goals and achievements will change. Optimistic self-views can improve performance: in this sense, the present

[3] For example, in Loewenstein (1996), people in a "cold" state (i.e., not hungry, angry, in pain, etc.) underestimate the influence of a future "hot" state (i.e., craving, angry, jealous, sad, etc.). He argues that this underestimation of future visceral drives is due to constrained memory for visceral experiences.

[4] Reasoning is done deliberately, but intuitive thoughts seem to come spontaneously to mind.

model is also related to Bénabou and Tirole (2002) and Compte and Postlewait (2004). However, our focus is different from theirs because the self is considered to be immersed in a variety of motives.People may have the motives to direct self-relevant information processing in favor of the confirmation and validation of existing self-beliefs. There may be a cultural regime that generates a x-inefficient economy (Altman, 2001). X-inefficiency stems from an actual preference for less competitive cultural norms. In the theory of x-efficiency, individuals produce less than they might under relatively good conditions.

Teraji (2009) considers an economic agent who faces a sequence of decisions over a horizon of two periods: $t = 0, 1$. In each period, the agent selects some level of effort.At $t = 0$, "Self 0,"which represents the actual self, is activated.At $t = 1$, "Self 1,"which represents the ideal self, can be activated. At the beginning of $t = 1$, the agent has to make a judgment about the relative merits of options he / she is about to face. Then the agent chooses one of two options: one is to choose Self 0, and the other is to choose Self 1.

The timing is as follows:

At $t = 0$:

- Self 0 exerts effort in the process of production.
- The payoff is realized.

At $t = 1$:

- Judgments are done based on the agent's chances of activating Self 1.
- The agent chooses Self 0 or Self 1.
- Self 0 or Self 1 exerts effort in the process of production.
- The payoff is realized.

At $t = 0$, the agent starts with Self 0. At $t = 1$, self-concepts may be largely idiosyncratic. Self-confidence or self-esteem refers to the extent to which individuals see themselves as having control over their own outcomes. The decision to change oneself is the outcome of appraisal, in which the agent assesses how effective Self 1 would be and how successfully he / she could activate it. A self-serving bias exists when an individual's preferences affect his / her beliefs in an optimistic direction. The agent may have some self-serving bias for the emergence of Self 1. In our model, optimism depends on the agent's prediction of how successfully he / she activates Self 1. The agent may be biased in the assessment of the probability of successful self-change.

Let λ be the subjective belief that the agent activates Self 1 successfully in period 1. Thus, with probabilityλ the agent predicts the emergence of Self 1, and with probability $1-\lambda$ the agent predicts that Self 0 remains in period 1. The level of self-confidence thus transforms into his / her subjective beliefs over λ. With this formulation, $\lambda=0$ means no self-serving bias. The manifestation of self-serving bias is optimism about one's own future prospects to activate Self 1. If $\lambda>0$, the agent may have some self-serving bias;the larger is λ (or the smaller is $1-\lambda$),the stronger is the self-serving bias. People with no self-serving bias stick to Self 0 at $t = 1$.

At $t = 1$, Self 1 can produce output with the following technology:

1 with probabilityπE,

and

0 with probability $1-\pi E$,

where E is the level of effort that Self 1 chooses in period 1, and $0 <\pi < 1$ is a parameter. Thus, the production activity is either a success or a failure. Self 1 will receive 1 in case of success and 0 in case of failure.

At $t = 0, 1$, Self 0 can produce output with the following technology:

1 with probability$\theta\pi e_t$,

and

0 with probability $1-\theta\pi e_t$,

where e_t is the level of effort that Self 0 chooses at $t = 0, 1$, and $0 <\theta < 1$ is a parameter. In each t, Self 0 will receive 1 in case of success and 0 in case of failure. Self 1 has greater chances of succeeding than Self 0 in period 1.

Self 1's flow payoff at $t = 1$, V, is given by:

$$V = \pi E - (1/2)E^2,$$

where $(1/2)E^2$ is the cost of effort, which measures the task's difficulty. The first order condition with respect to the level of effort is $E = \pi$. Thus, at the end of $t = 1$, Self 1 obtains:

$$V = (1/2)\,\pi^2.$$

Likewise, Self 0's flow payoff at $t = 0, 1$, U_t, is given by:

$$U_t = \theta\pi e_t - (1/2)\,e_t^2,$$

where $(1/2)\,e_t^2$ is the cost of effort at $t = 0, 1$. Self 0 supplies the amount of effort as follows: $e_t = \theta\pi$. Self 0 always exerts less effort than Self 1. At the end of $t = 0, 1$, Self 0 obtains:

$$U_t = (1/2)(\theta\pi)^2.$$

Discrepancies between Self 0 and Self 1 produce dejection-related emotions (depression, disappointment, or sadness) in period 1. Let c a (dejection-related) psychological cost to maintain Self 0 in period 1. That is, the agent suffers the cost c if he / she chooses Self 0 at $t = 1$. In the following analysis, it is assumed that $(1/2)(\theta\pi)^2 > c$.

On the contrary, incoherent self-concepts might result in distress because people feel some kind of uncertainty regarding their self-image. People have feelings of coherence. Self-verification involves the impulse to act in accordance with the self-concept. The psychological significance of the stable self-views can be appreciated by considering what happens to individuals whose self-views have been changed. Let d a disutility cost that the agent attaches to any self-change at $t = 1$. That is, choosing Self 1 involves the cost d in period 1. In the following analysis, it is assumed that $(1/2)\pi^2 > d$.

Thus, at the end of $t = 1$, with probability λ the agent expects to obtain $V - d$; with probability $1 - \lambda$ the agent expects to obtain $U_1 - c$.

At $t = 1$, the agent decides whether to choose Self 1 or not, having the subjective beliefs over λ (defining the self-serving bias). Formally, let x denote the probability that the agent (who may have some self-serving bias) chooses Self 1 in period 1.

The agent's utility as of period 0 is denoted by:

$$U_0 = (1/2)(\theta\pi)^2.$$

The expected utility perceived by the agent (who may have some self-serving bias) at the beginning of $t = 1$, W_1, is:

$$W_1 = x\lambda(V - d) + (1 - x)(1 - \lambda)(U_1 - c).$$

Then, the expected utility, W_1, isdenoted by:

$$W_1 = x\lambda\{(1/2)\,\pi^2 - d\} + (1 - x)(1 - \lambda)\{(1/2)(\theta\pi)^2 - c\}.$$

The agent (who may have some self-serving bias) at the beginning of period 1chooses the probability$x$ so as to solve:

$$\begin{aligned} W_1 &= \max_x x\lambda\{(1/2)\,\pi^2 - d\} + (1 - x)(1 - \lambda)\{(1/2)(\theta\pi)^2 - c\} \\ &= \max_x x[\lambda\{(1/2)\,\pi^2 - d\} - (1 - \lambda)\{(1/2)(\theta\pi)^2 - c\}] \\ &\qquad + (1 - \lambda)\{(1/2)(\theta\pi)^2 - c\}. \end{aligned}$$

This involves comparing the expected utility of Self 1, $\lambda\{(1/2)\,\pi^2 - d\}$, with the expected utility of Self 0, $(1 - \lambda)\{(1/2)(\theta\pi)^2 - c\}$. The former is larger the latter, the agent decides to choose Self 1, that is, $x = 1$. Changing oneself is thus one option. The former is smaller than the latter, the agent decides to choose Self 0, that is, $x = 0$. The former is equivalent to the latter, the agent is indifferent between Self 1 and Self 0.

Or, equivalently,

$$x = 1 \qquad \text{if } \lambda > \lambda^*,$$

and

$$x = 0 \qquad \text{if } \lambda < \lambda^*,$$

where

$$\lambda^* = \frac{\frac{1}{2}(\theta\pi)^2 - c}{\frac{1}{2}\pi^2 - d + \frac{1}{2}(\theta\pi)^2 - c}$$

Thus, the agent whose prediction is $\lambda > \lambda^*$ decides to choose Self 1, that is, $x = 1$. On the other hand, the agent whose prediction is $\lambda < \lambda^*$ decides to choose Self 0, that is, $x = 0$. If $\lambda = \lambda^*$, x may take any value in [0, 1]. Intentional self-change depends on the agent's self-confidence.

Then, the expected utility perceived by the individual at the beginning of period 1 is rewritten as:

$$W_1 = \begin{cases} \lambda\{(1/2)\,\pi^2 - d\} & \text{if } \lambda > \lambda^*, \\ (1-\lambda)\{(1/2)(\theta\pi)^2 - c\} & \text{if } \lambda < \lambda^*, \end{cases}$$

when the activity is undertaken in period 1. At the beginning of period 1, the agent, whose prediction λ is above λ^*, expects to obtain the utility $\lambda\{(1/2)\,\pi^2 - d\}$. On the other hand, the agent, whose prediction λ is below λ^*, then expects to obtain the utility $(1-\lambda)\{(1/2)(\theta\pi)^2 - c\}$.

People are influenced by two factors, self-enhancement and self-verification. Psychological costs then contribute to increasing or decreasing λ^*. In this model, c (a psychological cost to maintain Self 0) and d (a disutility cost that the agent attaches to intentional self-change) affect λ^*. The agent suffers the cost c if he / she sticks to Self 0 in period 1 (self-discrepancy). On the contrary, the agent might prefer to have the coherent self-image. Then, choosing Self 1 in period 1 involves the cost d (self-verification). It follows that:

$$\partial\lambda^*/\partial c < 0,$$

and

$$\partial\lambda^*/\partial d > 0.$$

Thus, λ^* is decreasing in c, and it is increasing in d. There is an inert area within which a person does not change from Self 0 to Self 1. It is the area of λ below λ^*, that is, the interval $[0, \lambda^*]$. The agent with $\lambda < \lambda^*$ sticks to Self 0 in period 1. Self-discrepancy results in depression. The greater the psychological cost$c$ associated with the actual-ideal discrepancy then decreases the inert area ($\partial\lambda^*/\partial c < 0$). People who hold more positive expectancies for themselves (self-enhancement) can cope effectively with stressful situations. Self-enhancers are more likely to overestimate the actual-ideal discrepancy for desired behavioral change. Overestimating the psychological cost c associated with dissonance, they are more likely to be motivated to change themselves. On the contrary, self-verification undermines intentional self-change. Self-verifying feedback leads to more stable self-concept. The self-serving bias exists when an individual overestimates the discrepancies between the actual self and the ideal self. Furthermore, the individual with some self-serving bias tends to underestimate the psychological cost d to intentional self-change. Then, the greater the psychological cost d to self-change increases the inert area ($\partial\lambda^*/\partial d > 0$). If people overestimate the psychological cost d, they are less likely to be motivated to change themselves.

The self is thus an adaptive process. It can be affected by two factors, self-enhancement and self-verification. People sometimes seek positive or self-enhancing feedback.If the self-enhancement effect is sufficiently large, Self 1 will be activated in the future. On the other hand,people may have a "passion for truth."People sometimes seek subjectively accurate or self-verifying feedback. If the self-verification effect is sufficiently large, Self 0 may persist. Self-verification solidifies and strengthens self-views. When the ideal self-guides are brought to mind, people will evaluate their behavior in terms of its fit to their own self-expectations for competent conduct. The self is motivated to maintain a certain kind of self-enhancement effect or self-verification effect.

Standard economic theory is based on the assumption that people can identify and choose what is optimal for them. Can people really choose what is best for them? The inert area idea permits both optimal and sub-optimal economic results within the same framework. Economic variables are subject to inertia. X-inefficiency is the gap between observed performance and existing best performance (Leibenstein, 1979). The assumption of effort variability is critical to x-efficiency theory. The degree of x-efficiency is linked with λ, the subjective belief that the agent successfully activates Self 1. What level of effort an individual exerts depends on some critical valueλ^*. The low-effort level persists for one subset of values of λ, where $(0 \leq)\ \lambda < \lambda^*$. On the other hand, Self 1 exerts the high-effort level for another subset of values of λ, where $(1 \geq)\ \lambda > \lambda^*$.X-efficiency is obtained only under high levels of self-confidence. Once such self-confidence is reduced, no intentional self-change is likely to occur. The conventional wisdom assumes that effort inputs must be maximized. However, for x-inefficiency to exist, effort must be a discretionary variable. Economic agents have the capacity to choose the quantity and quality of effort supplied in the process of production. Therefore, they would be producing below their potential or x-inefficiently.

Relationships with other people make possible the formation of one's self-image. Self-verification may occur when people choose partners who see them as they see themselves, thereby creating social environments that are likely to support their self-views. People perceive and form appraisals of other people around them. Appraisals enable individuals to adjust their behavior to the abilities and tendencies of their interaction partners. Behavioral change should foster self-concept change. The experimental evidence supports that individuals may have self-regarding preferences and other-regarding preferences in the structure of social interactions (Camerer and Fehr, 2006). The fact that we do not observe other-regarding behavior in the specified context does not mean that other-regarding preferences are absent.

The "egocentric" perspective does not portray altruism as genuine sympathy (Khalil, 2004).[5]The standard economic approach assumes that all behavior results from maximizing utility functions that depend on different commodities. The egocentric view, affiliated with Becker (1976), argues that the altruist helps the other because the utility function of the other is embedded in the altruist's. Self-interested behavior and altruism are not inconsistent for utility-maximizing individuals. The altruist derives pleasure not because the other is assisted but rather because the other's pleasure is already part of the altruist's utility.[6]Thus, the donor would give if this donation increases his/ her pleasure more by watching the pleasure of others. Altruistic behavior is caused by the fact that, as a factor in his / her utility function, the person also has the utility of the individuals whom he/ she wants to benefit.Altman (2005) argues that what individuals maximize is rather beside the point for Becker. An individual's utility might very well be maximized in terms of altruistic, moralistic, and ethical behavior. What counts in Becker's analytical framework is that individuals are rational given their objectives and the constraints. In Becker's framework, self-interest rationality is a subset of possible rational behavioral choices afforded to individuals.

The mechanisms of "fellow-feeling" are fundamental properties of human nature. In the language of modern psychology, fellow-feeling is a mechanism which connects individuals' affective or psychological states which are perceived as pleasurable or painful (Bardsley and Sugden, 2006). Fellow-feeling represents a kind of interdependence of feeling. Through fellow-feeling, each person's psychological states are influenced by his / her perceptions of the psychological states of others. One person *i*'s fellow-feeling

---

[5] Khalil (2004) critically examines major attempts by economists to model altruistic behavior as the outcome of optimization. Khalil offers an account of theories that account for altruism as reciprocity, as a source of vicarious satisfaction or as an evolutionary trait respectively.

[6] Altruism is frequently invoked by economists to explain relations between family members (Barro, 1974).

for another person *j* is to be understood as *i*'s lively consciousness of some psychological state of*j*'s, such that*j*'s consciousness has similar psychological qualities to *i*'s state. Formal models of social preferences assume that people are self-interested, but are also concerned about the payoffs of others (Rabin, 1993). That is, a player's utility function not only depends on his / her material payoff, but may also be a function of the allocation of resources within his / her reference group.Rabin (1993) argues that beliefs and intentions play a crucial role when individuals are motivated by reciprocity considerations.Reciprocity is the behavioral response to an action that is perceived as either kind or unkind. Whether an action is perceived to be kind or unkind depends on the fairness or unfairness of the intention underlying the action. When an individual wants to be kind to someone who was kind to him / her, and unkind to unkind persons, he / she has to assess the kindness (or unkindness) of his / her own action as well as that of others.Rabin (1993) adopts the framework of psychological game theory, developed by Geanakoplos, Pearce, and Stacchetti (1989). Psychological games differ from standard games in that a player's payoff depends not only on what strategy profile is played, but possibly also on what are the player's beliefs about other players' strategic choices or beliefs.Intentions matter for the perception of kindness and the corresponding reciprocation. Since the model involves belief-dependent motivations, the utility functions have to be defined on a larger domain than in standard game theory where payoffs depend on actions only. There can be many equilibria, depending on the beliefs the players happen to have. It becomes impossible to predict which equilibrium will be played since the model applies no constraint on possible beliefs.Inequality aversion means that people resist outcomes that are perceived as inequitable. The model of Fehr and Schmidt (1999) intends to capture the idea that an individual may be uneasy, to a certain extent, about the presence of inequality, even though he/she benefits from the unequal distribution.In the gift exchange game, Fehr, Kirchsteiger, and Riedl (1993) design competitive goods market experiments that allow for the emergence of reciprocal interactions. Buyers make a "gift" to the sellers by paying prices above the competitive level. Sellers in turn respond reciprocally by choosing quality levels above what is dictated by their pecuniary interests.

The mixture of heterogeneous preferences is likely to create profound effects on aggregate behavior because individuals explicitly take heterogeneity and incentive interactions between different types of others into account. For David Hume (1739–40 [1985]), rationality is phenomena that reason discovers in emergent institutions. Rules of justice originate as regularities in behavior in relation to human interaction. On Hume's account, once the necessary expectations are in place, conventions are self-enforcing.[7] Certain kinds of common understandings among individuals are then required to produce the common associations of ideas that allow conventions to emerge and to reproduce themselves.Norms are a special kind of expectation. People are, to some degree, motivated by a desire to meet other peoples' expectations, and to act according to conventions that have become established. Norms that serve as the benchmark for evaluating behavior may vary from one culture to another. The norms of fairness are thus culturally variable. The evolutionary dynamics accounting for cooperation include the proliferation of behaviors as the result of social learning from others as well as the genetic transmission of information from parents to offspring. Gintis, Henrich, Bowles, Boyd, and Fehr (2008) argue that human morality is the product of gene-culture coevolution. Genetic adaptation can produce psychological traits designed to enhance one's success to the environment where pro-sociality is highly rewarded. However, only a purely genetic approach cannot explain the degree of pro-social behavior observed in humans. A co-evolutionary process between cultural and genetic transmission is at work. Gene-culture coevolution is a form of niche construction theory in which cultural rules create a group structure that affects individual fitness. Gene-culture coevolution produces not only highly social creatures but creatures whose pro-sociality is genetically encoded.

---

[7] According to Lewis (1969 [2002]), a convention is a regular pattern of behavior that is a strict Nash equilibrium in a coordination game.

Chapter 5

EVOLUTION OF SOCIAL PREFERENCES

5.1. EVOLUTION

In certain conditions, altruistic behavior can emerge and prevail. The behavior of an individual can be determined both by genetic inheritance and cultural one (Bergstrom and Stark, 1993). In evolutionary settings all depend on the complexities of the situations in which evolution takes place. Altruism can prevail when individuals are likely to interact with others who share the same role model.

Bester and Güth (1998) show that, in a strategic interaction context, altruism may be favored by evolution. In their model, all members in a population interact with each other in pairs. Under the model specification, the altruist who encounters an egoist can earn a larger profit than an egoist who encounters an egoist. The consequence is that altruism will spread out in the population.

In Bester and Güth's(1998) model, all members are identical in the population. Two players, player 1 and player 2, play a symmetric game with "material payoffs" given by:

$$U_1(y_1, y_2) = y_1\,(ky_2 + m - y_1),$$

and

$$U_2(y_1, y_2) = y_2\,(ky_1 + m - y_2),$$

where $y_1 \geq 0$ and $y_2 \geq 0$ are the strategies of player 1 and player 2, respectively, and $-1 < k < 1$ and $m > 0$ are parameters. Each player's success depends, not only on his / her own action, but also on the choice of the other player. If $k > 0$, the game exhibits "positive externalities" because a higher action by player i increases the success of player j. "Negative externalities" occur if $k < 0$. For example, in a production game with externalities, where y_1 and y_2 denote the players' effort or input decisions, player 1's success can be defined as the difference betweenhis / her output, $y_1 (ky_2 + m)$, and his / her (quadratic) effort cost, y_1^2.

Bester and Güth (1998) assume that the players do not necessarily maximize their material payoffs, but rather weighted sums of own and opponent's payoff. Player i's preferences are then described by:

$$V_i = \gamma U_i + (1-\gamma)\, U_j, \quad j \neq i.$$

Here the concern that player i expresses for player j is represented by the weight $1-\gamma$. If the preference parameter γ is smaller than 1, that is, $\gamma < 1$, player i is said to be altruistic. If $\gamma = 1$, player i is said to be egoistic.

When an altruist invades a population of egoists and performs better than his / her opponents, then altruism will spread out and eliminate egoistic behavior in the process of evolution. In what follows, $R(\gamma, \gamma')$ denotes a player's success when he / she has the preference parameter γ while his / her opponent has the preference parameter γ'. Then γ is restricted to the interval [1/2, 1]. By using the concept of evolutionarily stable strategies (ESS) (Maynard Smith, 1982), Bester and Güth (1998) define the evolutionary stability of a preference parameter γ^*, which lies in the interval [1/2, 1], as follows:

A preference parameter γ^* is called"evolutionarily stable" if

$$R(\gamma^*, \gamma^*) \geq R(\gamma, \gamma^*) \text{ for all } \gamma,$$

and

$$R(\gamma^*, \gamma) > R(\gamma, \gamma) \text{ whenever } R(\gamma^*, \gamma^*) = R(\gamma, \gamma^*).$$

According to the first requirement, an evolutionarily stable parameter γ^* is a best reply against itself. Then a population with parameter γ^* cannot be invaded by a small minority with deviant parameterγ. Furthermore, the second condition rules out that an alternative best reply, $\gamma \neq \gamma^*$, can spread out in the population if several parameters are equally successful. Bester and Güth (1998) provide the following results:

- Let $k > 0$. Then $\gamma^* = (2-k)/2$ is the unique evolutionarily stable preference parameter.
- Let $k < 0$. Then $\gamma^* = 1$ is the unique evolutionarily stable preference parameter.

These results imply that the sign of the strategic interaction in the material function (the sign of k) determines the evolutionarily stable preference parameter γ^*. In Bester and Güth's (1998) model, the critical condition is whether the game exhibits positive externalities or negative ones. In particular, as $\gamma^* < 1$, the level of altruism is positively related to the positive parameter k. Altruism becomes more important when the strategic interdependence between the players is relatively high; $k \rightarrow 1$ implies $\gamma^* \rightarrow 1/2$. Complementarity (positive strategic interaction) thus leads to the altruistic preference parameter in the evolutionary process. The ESS concept is based on the idea that higher success reflects an advantage in reproduction. In the case of positive externalities, it is beneficial for the altruist to induce his / her opponent to increase his / her action level. Thus, the altruist will succeed in invading a society of egoists. Their analysis, however, restricts the set of preferences, not allowing broader preference parameter regionssuch as envy as well as altruism. An envious person will value the material payoffs of relevant reference agents negatively. Human societies exhibit multiple stable equilibria with different mixes of altruistic and envious people, and different cultural rules enforcing behavioral norms.

5.2. SOCIAL PREFERENCES

Standard economic theory is built on the assumption that all people are exclusively self-interested and do not care about the well-being of other human beings. This assumption may be true for some, but it is certainly not true for all. Formal models of social preferences assume that people are self-interested, but are also concerned about the payoffs of others. That is, a player's utility function not only depends on his / her material payoff, but may also be a function of the allocation of resources within his / her reference group. More formally, given a group of N persons, let $x = (x_1, x_2, \ldots\ldots, x_N)$

denote an allocation of physical resources out of some set X of feasible allocations. The utility of individual i may be any function of the total allocation. The self-interested person i's utility only depends on x_i. Individual i has social preferences if, for any given x_i, person i's utility is affected by variations of $x_j, j \neq i$. A person is altruistic if the first partial derivatives of $u(x_1, x_2, \ldots, x_N)$ with respect to $x_1, x_2, \ldots, x_N$ are strictly positive.

In Charness and Rabin (2002), a two-person model of preferences assumes that player's propensity to sacrifice for another player is characterized by parameters: the weight on the other's payoff when he / she is ahead and the weight when he / she is behind. Letting x_i and x_j be player i's and player j's material payoffs, consider the following simple formulation of player i's preferences:

$$U_i(x_i, x_j) = (\rho r + \sigma s)x_j + (1 - \rho r - \sigma s)x_i, \quad i \neq j,$$

where

$r = 1$ if $x_j > x_i$, and $r = 0$ otherwise;

$s = 1$ if $x_j < x_i$, and $s = 0$ otherwise.

The weight i places on j's payoff may depend on whether j is getting a higher or lower payoff than i. The parameters ρ and σ allow for a range of different "distributional preferences." One form of distributional preferences is simple competitive preferences, which is represented by assuming that $\sigma \leq \rho \leq 0$. Then, people like their payoffs to be high relative to others' payoffs. Another form of distributional preferences is "inequality aversion," which corresponds to $\sigma < 0 < \rho < 1$. Then, player i likes material payoffs, and prefers that payoffs are equal. People prefer to minimize disparities between their own payoffs and those of other people.

Inequality aversion means that people resist outcomes that are perceived as inequitable. Then, people are willing to give up some material payoffs to move in the direction of more equitable outcomes. The model of Fehr and Schmidt (1999) intends to capture the idea that an individual may be uneasy, to a certain extent, about the presence of inequality, even though he / she benefits from the unequal distribution. Given a group of N persons, the Fehr-Schmidt (1999) utility function of player i is given by:

$$U_i(x_1,.....,x_N) = x_i - \frac{\alpha_i}{N-1}\sum_{j\neq i}\max|x_j - x_i, 0|$$
$$-\frac{\beta_i}{N-1}\sum_{j\neq i}\max|x_i - x_j, 0|,$$

where x_j denotes the material payoff person j gets, α_i is a parameter that measures how much player i dislikes disadvantageous inequality (an "envy" weight), and β_i measures how much i dislikes advantageous inequality (a "guilt" weight). It is assumed that $0 \leq \beta_i \leq \alpha_i$ and $\beta_i < 1$. That is, an agent dislikes advantageous inequality less than disadvantageous inequality ($0 \leq \beta_i \leq \alpha_i$), and an agent does not suffer terrible guilt when he / she is in a relatively good position ($\beta_i < 1$).

In the two-player case, the utility function is simplified to:

$$U_i(x_i, x_j) = x_i - \alpha_i \max|x_j - x_i, 0| - \beta_i \max|x_i - x_j, 0|, \quad i \neq j.$$

The second term in the utility function measures the utility loss from disadvantage inequality, while the third term measures the loss from advantageous inequality. Player i's utility function is rewritten as:

$$U_i(x_i, x_j) = \begin{cases} x_i - \alpha_i(x_j - x_i), & \text{if } x_j > x_i, \\ x_i - \beta_i(x_i - x_j), & \text{if } x_j < x_i, \end{cases}$$

where $0 \leq \beta_i \leq \alpha_i$ and $\beta_i < 1$. For two players, the Charness-Rabin (2002) distributional model has a similar piecewise linear form; their analysis emphasizes quasi-maximin preferences ($1 > \beta_i > -\alpha_i > 0$), and can accommodate competitive preferences ($\beta_i < 0 < \alpha_i$) as well as inequality-averse preferences ($\alpha_i > 0$, $\beta_i > 0$). Theories of inequality aversion have the merit of having some degree of experimental support (rejections of unequal offers in ultimatum games). Yet, how the context is framed would matter to an evaluation of outcomes. Norm-based behavior seems desirable in such contexts as group production settings. It seems reasonable to assume that the prevailing norms affect individuals' preferences. We need a theory in which individuals can be motivated by self-regarding or other-regarding preferences in the evolutionary process of norms.

5.3. Evolution of Social Preferences

The standard conception of the economic agent as a creature driven by material self-interest has provided powerful theoretical tools in the analysis of diverse problems. However, experimental support for this conception has been fragile. Results from experiments on public goods games, ultimatum games, trust games, and gift exchange games demonstrate that people in fact deviate from self-interest in systematic ways.[1] Aside from being concerned with their own payoffs, subjects appear to be concerned also with the payoffs of others. Preferences having this property are referred to as being "social interdependent"or "other-regarding." The contents of self-interest are usually not specified by economic theory. Self-interest is not all of human motivation, and it should be recognized as a special case. Departures from the standard self-interest assumption are potentially important for behavioral economic analysis of the self.

In economics, an individual is assumed to be calculating how to maximize his / her own exogenously given utility, independently of any psychological factor. In real life, however, people are affected by psychological and emotional factors. People feel loyalty or jealousy in society, which appears in economic literature only rarely.[2] Emotions generate behavior. An "internal norm" is a pattern of behavior enforced in part by internal sanctions, including shame, guilt, and loss of self-esteem, as opposed to purely external sanctions, such as material rewards and punishments (Gintis, 2003). Neglecting these psychological factors creates serious risk that economists may not understand the diversity of norms and the changes in economic performances that are induced by changes in norms.

The conjunction of: (a) a postulated genetic basis for human behavioral predispositions, and (b) the demonstrable impact of environment on phenotypic variation in behavior, opens up the possibility of a scientific research program for studying the influence of human environments on human preferences (Ben-Ner and Putterman, 2000). The research endogenizes preferences to economic and social environments.[3] Biologists distinguish between a genotype, the underlying genetic constitution of an organism, and a phenotype, the developed organism including behavioral propensities. An

[1] See, for example, Isaac and Walker (1988).

[2] See Elster (1998) and Frank (1988) for links between emotions and economic behavior.

[3] See also Lévy-Garboua, Meidinger, and Rapoport (2006) for the mechanisms whereby a variety of social preferences are determined in a variety of social contexts.

organism's phenotype is determined by its genotype and the effect of environmental factors. Genotypes are mapped onto phenotypes. Evolution by natural selection acts differently on the phenotypes, which modifies the composition of the population. Similarly, human beings are influenced by the environments. If humans adjust phenotypes in response to their environments, they are almost unique in their ability to culturally transmit the acquired phenotypes to the next generation. Culture is thus as an aspect of human phenotypes and as a system for the transmission and selection of traits in its own right.Humans internalize norms through socialization. Society's values are transmitted through the internalization of norms. If the norms, promoted by internalization, are altruistic, then individuals will behave altruistically. An altruistic act is motivated by a concern for the well-being or interests of others.

Cultural transmission leads people to internalize norms in environments. Norms are informal; norms are public and shared, but they may not be enforced at all. In particular, conformity to a norm is conditional on expectations about other peoples' behavior andbeliefs. Norms are often considered to be the historical legacy of a traditional culture supported and adhered to in society. The internalization of norms can guide not only the behavior, but also the goals of action. The influence of culture on the decision-making process can be associated to the concept of "bounded rationality" elaborated by Herbert Simon (1959, 1993). There is then a gap between actual behavior and the predictions of rational agent models. As a result of gaps, humans have a tendency to respect norms. Gintis (2003) offers the framework to model Herbert Simon's explanation of altruism. According to Simon, altruistic norms can "hitchhike" on the general tendency of internal norms to be personally fitness enhancing. Simon defines docility as a willingness to be taught or to defer to the superior knowledge of others. Evolutionary models, not based on kinship, demonstrate how altruistic traits, such as Simon calls docility, can have survival value. Gintis (2003) shows that if the internalization of some norms is personally fitness-enhancing, then genes promoting the capacity to internalize can evolve. Given this genetic capacity, altruistic norms will be internalized as well. The internalization of norms permits rapid cultural adaptation towards fitness-maximization, while a purely genetic adaptive process would have taken orders of magnitude longer in time. Altruism thus hitchhikes on the personal fitness-enhancing capacity of norm internalization.

An organization enjoys good performance as a result of high morale and suffers bad performance as a result of low morale. The economic performance of an organization can vary because of the team atmosphere that prevails.

However, in contract theory and principal-agent theory, which are based on material (pecuniary) incentives, values and preferences are taken as given. Thus, the existing literature on incentives cannot offer a way of explaining the diversity of morale observed across organizations. There is something other than material incentives that matters in organizations.

In Teraji (2007), the process by which norms evolve exhibits generalized increasing returns. First, groups appear to be quite internally "heterogeneous" with respect to norms. If the norm, which is enforced by altruism, persists in the limit, everyone chooses the high effort level and high morale is sustainable. On the other hand, if the norm, which is enforced by envy, is persistent, everyone chooses the low effort level and the performance decays in the long run.

In Teraji's (2007) model, given a group of N persons, each individual j chooses his / her effort level, e_j (≥ 0). Suppose that output is some function of each agent's effort, given by $F(\mathbf{e})$, where $\mathbf{e}$ is an N-dimensional vector of agents' effort levels. Consider a work situation in which each agent's compensation is determined as $F(\mathbf{e})/N$. It is painful to put forth effort, and the pain that an agent feels is given by $c(e_j)$ that is exogenous, where $c' > 0$ and $c''> 0$.

Agent i's utility function is given by:

$$U_i(\mathbf{e};\mu_i) = \frac{F(\mathbf{e})}{N} - c(e_i) + \mu_i\ (N-1)\ \frac{F(\mathbf{e})}{N}.$$

The first two terms of the right-hand side for agent i's utility function capture self-interest, and the last term represents other-regarding preferences. The parameter μ_i is the weight (or the"binding powerof the internal norm") that agent i's preferences put on all other agents' well-being. Also, $(N-1)F(\mathbf{e})/N$ is the aggregate compensations of all agents other than i in the N-member group under consideration. The last term is an attempt to formalize the discussion of internal normswhich are social and endogenous.

Suppose there are two possible types of norms that can be internalized by individuals. We say that agent i's internal norm is enforced by "altruism" if $\mu_i \equiv \mu^+ > 0$. With the binding power of this sort, i's utility is an increasing function of the compensations of other agents. On the other hand, we say that i's internal norm is enforced by"envy" if $\mu_i \equiv \mu^- < 0$.[4] Then, i's utility is a

[4] For the following analysis, we assume that $|\mu^-| \leq 1/(N-1)$.

decreasing function of the compensations of others. Initially, each agent is endowed with a particular norm.

Each agent chooses his / her effort level, given the parameter μ_i. As the utility function U_i is strictly concave in e_i and the efforts are continuous, there would be a unique utility maximizer for U_i. High (or low) effort level corresponds to high (or low) morale in the group. We present an equilibrium concept somewhat different from the standard Nash equilibrium of a game; given the binding power of i's internal normμ_i, an effort profile$\mathbf{e}^*$ is a morale equilibrium if:

$$U_i(\mathbf{e}^*; \mu_i) \geq U_i(e_i, \mathbf{e}^*_{-i}; \mu_i),$$

for all agents i and alle_i.

A morale equilibrium holds so that each agent takes others' effort levels as given. It is necessary to compare morale equilibria, one with μ^+ and one with μ^-. We show that equilibrium effort is higher with μ^+ (> 0) than it would be with μ^- (< 0).

To make our analysis simple, we assume that $F(\mathbf{e}) = \sum_j e_jandc(e_i) = e_i^2/2$. Thus, we have:

$$U_i(\mathbf{e}; \mu_i) = \frac{\sum_j e_j}{N} - \frac{e_j^2}{2} + \mu_i\ (N-1)\ \frac{\sum_j e_j}{N}.$$

Teraji (2007)investigates the evolution of norms that are acquired and internalized through socialization in the group. The model represents each individual's updating as a process of switching from one norm to another one through learning from other agents. It introduces the socio-economic interaction between individuals in the group. At the beginning of time t, the number of agents with trait μ^+ (> 0), i.e., the binding power of the internal norm enforced by altruism, is denoted by n_t. Let τ_t be the fraction of individuals with trait μ^+ at the beginning of time t, i.e., $\tau_t = n_t/N$. Thus, the fraction of individuals with trait μ^- (< 0), i.e., the binding power of the internal norm which is enforced by envy, is $1-\tau_t = (N-n_t)/N$ at the beginning of t.

Teraji (2007) formulates a random-matching model in the group, which introduces chance events that affect population dynamics through socialization. Individuals try to socialize themselves to particular norms at the beginning of each time. Socialization occurs as follows. With a certain probability of socialization, agent i is matched with an individual in the group and then adopts the norm of that individual. The probability of socialization is allowed to depend on the fraction of individuals in the group. In Teraji's (2007) model, socialization acts as a type of"complementarities."[5] That is, an agent with trait μ^- (or μ^+) has more incentives to socialize with an individual with trait μ^+ (or μ^-) as μ^+ (or μ^-) is the more widely dominant one in the group. Specifically, socialization to agent i with trait μ^-in time$t$occurs with probability $q(\tau_t)$, which is a continuous, strictly increasingfunction in τ_t. On the other hand, socialization to agent i with trait μ^+ in time$t$occurs with probability $q(1-\tau_t)$, which is a continuous, strictly increasing function in $1-\tau_t$. With probability $1 - q(\tau_t)$ or $1 - q(1-\tau_t)$, agent i does not get randomly matched with somebody else in the group. Moreover, it is assumed that $q_0 = 0$ and $q_1 =$ 1.

Let P^{+-} denote the transmission probability that an agent with trait μ^+ is socialized to trait μ^- at the end of time t. The socialization mechanism is then characterized by the following transition probability:

$$P^{+-} = q(1-\tau_t)\left(\frac{N-n_t}{N-1}\right).$$

This represents the coefficient of norm transmission, where an agent with trait μ^+ (at the beginning of t) is matched with an individual with trait μ^- of the remaining individuals, and adopts and internalizes that trait at the end of t. The transition probability, P^{++}, that an agent with μ^+ sticks to that trait in the socialization mechanism is given by:

$$P^{++} = 1 - q(1-\tau_t) + q(1-\tau_t)\left(\frac{n_t - 1}{N-1}\right).$$

In the term $1 - q(1 - \tau_t)$ of the right-hand side, an agent with μ^+ does not get matched with somebody else in the group and sticks to that trait in t. In the last term, an agent with μ^+ at the beginning of t has a chance of socialization, but is matched with an individual with μ^+ of the remaining individuals in the group (the agent does not change his / her trait).

Similarly, for an agent with trait μ^- at the beginning of t, we get:

---

[5] In Bisin and Verdier (2001), the interior rest point under cultural complementarities is unstable while the other rest points are stable.

$$P^{-+} = q(\tau_t)\left(\frac{n_t}{N-1}\right),$$

$$P^{--} = 1 - q(\tau_t) + q(\tau_t)\left(\frac{N-n_t-1}{N-1}\right).$$

Given these transmission probabilities, the fraction τ_{t+1} of individuals with trait μ^+ at the beginning of time $t + 1$ is calculated to be:

$$\tau_{t+1} = \tau_t + P^{-+}(1 - \tau_t) - P^{+-}\tau_t.$$

Substituting these equations, we obtain:

$$\tau_{t+1} - \tau_t = \{(N - n_t)/(N - 1)\}\ \tau_t\{q(\tau_t) - q(1 - \tau_t)\}.$$

This is the equation for the population dynamics through socialization. Teraji (2007) derives conditions that guarantee that the population dynamics converges to a "homogeneous" population in the limit. Assume that $\tau_0 > 1/2$ holds initially. Then, we have $\partial(\tau_{t+1} - \tau_t) / \partial\tau_t > 0$. Thus, we have $\tau_t \to 1$ for any $\tau_0 > 1/2$. Everyone adopts the same norm eventually. Similarly, the dynamics implies that $\tau_t \to 0$ for any $\tau_0 < 1/2$. The process by which norms evolve through socialization thus exhibits generalized increasing returns. Social norms take the form of conventions, i.e., the modes of behavior to which a majority of agents subscribe. People follow a certain norm through socialization. In the presence of generalized increasing returns, chance events have large and persistent effects due to positive feedbacks. In the self-enforcing process that depends on the initial prevalence of norms, only one social norm emerges. The social norm, which is enforced by altruism or envy, persists in the long run if a majority of agents adopt that norm in the group initially. In the socialization mechanism, individuals behave in conformity with a particular social norm eventually.

Agent *i*'s utility function, whose binding power of the internal norm is μ^+ or μ^- at the beginning of time t, is given by:

$$U_i(\mathbf{e}_t;\mu^+) = \frac{\sum_j e_{jt}}{N} - \frac{e_{jt}^2}{2} + (P^{++}\ \mu^+ + P^{+-}\ \mu^-)\ (N-1)\ \frac{\sum_j e_{jt}}{N},$$

$$U_i(\mathbf{e}_t;\mu^-) = \frac{\sum_j e_{jt}}{N} - \frac{e_{jt}^2}{2} + (P^{-+}\ \mu^+ + P^{--}\ \mu^-)\ (N-1)\ \frac{\sum_j e_{jt}}{N}.$$

Agent i chooses i's effort level at the end of each time. In Teraji (2007), there is a unique effort level maximizing the utility function. The utility-maximizing effort levels for agent i in t, $e^*_{i\,t}(\mu^+)$ and $e^*_{i\,t}(\mu^-)$, are given by:

$$e^*_{i\,t}(\mu^+) = \frac{1}{N} + (P^{++}\ \mu^+ + P^{+-}\ \mu^-)\ \frac{N-1}{N},$$

and

$$e^*_{i\,t}(\mu^-) = \frac{1}{N} + (P^{-+}\ \mu^+ + P^{--}\ \mu^-)\ \frac{N-1}{N}.$$

Suppose that $\tau_0 > 1/2$ holds in the group initially. Then, $\tau_t \rightarrow 1$ in the limit. Thus, we have $P^{++} \rightarrow 1$ and $P^{+-} \rightarrow 0$. And, it holds that $e^*_{i\,t}(\mu^+) \rightarrow \{1 + \mu^+ (N-1)\}/N$. Furthermore, $n_t/(N-1) \rightarrow 1$ and $(N - n_t - 1)/(N-1) \rightarrow 0$ for the remaining individuals other than agent i. Then, we have $P^{-+} \rightarrow 1$ and $P^{--} \rightarrow 0$. Thus, we have $e^*_{it}(\mu^-) \rightarrow \{1+ \mu^+ (N-1)\}/N$ in the limit. Similarly, if $\tau_0 < 1/2$ holds in the group initially, we have $e^*_{it}(\mu^+) \rightarrow \{1+ \mu^- (N-1)\}/N$ and $e^*_{it}(\mu^-) \rightarrow \{1+ \mu^- (N-1)\}/N$ in the limit.

Morale is norm-based motivation. The social norm generates the equilibrium effort level in the long run. Everyone chooses the same effort level in equilibrium because of a particular norm that prevails in society. When there are multiple equilibria, these equilibria can be ranked. Morale is higher in the high-effort equilibrium than in the low-effort equilibrium. Thus, we have two moraleequilibria; in one equilibrium with high morale, every agent's effort level is $\{1 + \mu^+(N-1)\}/N$, and in the other equilibrium with low morale, every agent's effort level is $\{1 + \mu^-(N-1)\}/N$, where $\mu^+>0>\mu^-$.

The process by which norms evolve through socialization is self-enforcing, and depends on the initial distribution of individuals with certain norms in the group. In this formulation, different norms typically exhibit different moraleequilibria in the long run. If the norm is enforced by altruism, every agent chooses the high equilibrium effort level in the long run. In this morale equilibrium, every agent is able to maintain high morale. Thus, norms inculcated through socialization can lead members to create incentives withinthe organizational context. On the other hand, if the norm, which is enforced by envy, persists, the low equilibrium effort level can be sustained. In this morale equilibrium, everyone shirks. Then, we have the decay of economic performance in the long run. Thus, the economic performance can vary depending on the norm that prevails withinthe organizational context.

A key finding of path dependence is a property of "lock-in" by historical events (Arthur, 1994). In a world of increasing returns to scale, initial and trivial circumstances can have important and irreversible influences on the ultimate market allocation of resources. The form of path dependence conflicts with the neoclassical model, where efficientoutcomes are attained. Why does an inefficient outcome persist? Where there is a feasible improvement to be gained from moving onto a better path, economic agents will be willing to pay to bring the improvement about. This issue has been addressed by Liebowitz and Margolis (1990, 1994).

In our formulation, effort depends on theprevailing norm within an organization. In a world of effort discretion, the economic performance can vary across organizations. Furthermore, the process by which norms evolve through socialization exhibits generalized increasing returns. One social norm emerges in the process that depends on the initial prevalence of norms. The social norm, enforced by altruism or envy, persists in the long run. Individuals try to socialize themselves to one particular norm. Which norm is persistent determines the equilibrium effort level. It is possible for low-effort organizations to survive in the long run. Then, the norm, enforced by envy, can be a cause of economic inefficiency. If the norm is enforced by envy, there does not exist the private incentives for individuals to choose the high-effort equilibrium. In a world where norms are determinants to effort levels, the path-dependent low-effort equilibrium can exist.

These discussions connect with what Harvey Leibenstein referred to as x-inefficiency. A large number of x-inefficiency studies exist, dating from Leibenstein (1966). He referred to the difference between maximal effectiveness of utilization and actual utilization as the degree of x-inefficiency. According toLeibenstein, individuals supply different amounts of effort, where effort is a multidimensional variable, under different organizational and environmental circumstances. Individual motivations and interactions between individuals are important. He presented a reasonable vision of human behavior within the organizational context, where x-inefficiency can persist stubbornly. Furthermore, Altman (2000) introduces effort discretion into the path-dependency modeling. In the world of path dependency, the free market typically generates sub-optimal long-run equilibrium solutions to a variety of economic problems, and the probability of sub-optimal equilibrium outcomes increases where increasing returns prevail. Given effort discretion, the quantity and quality of effort can vary. Labor productivity is affected by the quantity and quality of effort inputted into the process of production. In a world of effort discretion, private economic incentives need not exist for economic agents to adopt superior economic regimes. The introduction of effort variability allows for the existence of path-dependent high and low productivity firms in the long run.The existence of high and low productivity regimes might be a product of history, of random or deliberate actions taken sometime in the past.

Neoclassical economics remains firmly grounded in the two fundamental theorems of welfare economics. The first asserts that any perfectly competitive outcome is Pareto optimal. The second asserts that any Pareto optimal outcome may be achieved as a competitive equilibrium with the proper lump sum transfers. Altman (2005) argues that contemporary economic theory simply stresses the potential tradeoff between ethical behavior and the material well-being of the individual. Ethical behavior needs not be materially costly, but it is often so regarded in the literature. Adherence to norms are motivated not only by the material well-being, but also by internal, non-material well-being. People may follow norms simply because they feel uncomfortable, even in the absence of material sanctions, when they violate them.

Neoclassical economic theory predicts that ethical firms cannot survive in a competitive free market since it is assumed that such firms must produce at relatively higher unit costs.The neoclassical firms are producing as efficiently as possible given the objective constraints that they face. Economic agents are assumed to be self-regarding, especially with regards to maximizing their material welfare. Such narrowly self-interested behavior is a precondition of firms' long-term survival in the market economy. Inefficient firms cannot survive in a competitive market. If ethical behavior requires additional inputs into the process of production, the already efficient firm will generate higher unit costs or lower profits. The neoclassical firm is operating along the production possibility frontier. If the firm is assumed at maximum efficiency from the start, ethical behavior cannot contribute to the productivity of the firm.

In fact, Milton Friedman (1962) questions the ability of business managers to pursue the social interest.

> "If businessmen do have a social responsibility other than making maximum profits for stockholders, how are they to know what it is? Can self-selected private individuals decide what the social interest is? Can they decide how great a burden they are justified in placing on themselves or theirstockholdersto serve that social interest?" (1962, pp.133–4)

Instead, Friedman argues that a socially responsible firm is one that conducts the business in accord with stockholders' desires, which generally makes as much money as possible while conforms to the basic rules of the society. In Friedman's framework, firms are owned by stockholders who are principals, and business managers are agents with the duty to serve the interests of their principals. His position, based upon free-market ideology, has come under increasing attack since time of writing.Firms have responsibilities towards their environment that go beyond their legal and economic obligations. Within our economic system, there exists a growing cadre of companies where social, environmental, and ethical goals are on equal footing with the profit motive.

Anecdotal evidence suggests that there has been a shift in the breadth and nature of the perceived responsibilities of companies to the societies in which they operate. Corporate social responsibility (CSR) is the notion that companies are responsible not just to their stockholders, but also to other stakeholders (workers, suppliers, environmentalists, communities, etc.). Freeman's (1984) work helps to re-conceptualize the nature of the firm to encourage consideration of new external stakeholders, legitimizing new forms of managerial understanding and action. CSR should be understood as a broad concept, since it takes in the whole set philosophical and normative issues relating to the role of business in society, all the ethical obligations that maximize the positive impact of the firm on its social environment and minimize the negative impact. Organizations from this perspective are expected to manage responsibility in an extended web of stakeholder interests across increasingly permeable organization boundaries and to acknowledge a duty of care towards salient stakeholders, such as local communities and the environment. Business decisions are made by individuals or by committees, thus the ethics of business in reality are the ethics of the individuals who make business decisions. Of course, the actual behavior may be influenced by the culture of the organization.

Corporate identity ('what the company is') emerges from the interaction between the company and its consumers. Identity theory at the individual level has been used to explain role-related behavior. Social structures affect the extent to which an individual commits to a particular role. Corporate identity denotes the characteristic way in which an organization goes about its business, or how it behaves and interfaces with the social environment. Corporate behavior regarding ethical conformity, in light of normative expectations, represents a response mechanism to the social environment. Socialization, through which individuals learn the perspective necessary to perform roles, is expected to prime ethical identification. Corporate identity interplays with social concerns to influence the response to values, norms, and beliefs. Corporate social performance (CSP) is voluntary activities. Moral management yields CSP. Supplying CSP is not just like managing traditional market-based activities.CSP can be regarded as voluntary corporate commitment to exceed the explicit and implicit obligations imposed on a company by society's prevailing ideas and opinions. On the one hand, we have the interests of the economyarising from a largely unregulated market of companies pursuing their self-interest and on the other hand we have the interests of society arising from ethical or moral conformity that may suppress the effects of self-interest. Managers have to legitimate their activities within the field of tension between ethics and economic success. These aspects are strongly reflected in the dimensions of ethical or moral perceptions.

Chapter 6

CONCLUSION

Assumptions matter. The realism of assumptions is critical to revising the conventional theories and developing new ones.A conventional economic hypothesis stipulates that individuals behave as if they were seeking to maximize their material well-being, having full knowledge of the data needed in a virtually institution-free environment. In standard economic theory, the utility- or profit-maximization objective is dominant enough so that this single objective leads to good predictions. Then competitive market mechanisms can coordinate individual activities in an optimal manner. In fact, for Milton Friedman (1953), assumptions can never be realistic since they are abstractions from reality.[1]Important theories contain assumptions that might even be inaccurate descriptive representations of reality.For Friedman, what is important is that a set of admittedly unrealistic assumptions yields predictions of economic performance that are consistent with the conditions necessary for the survival of the firm in the market economy.Standard economic analysis, built on the assumptions of neoclassical theory, has little attention to ethics and morality beyond direct profit maximization.Efficiency, in the Pareto sense, is the main goal of the theory. The agency conception is based on the pecuniary conflict of interests of the principal (shareholder) and the agent (manager).In the neoclassical analytical framework, the market system creates a decision-making situation that favors practices to insure profit maximization

---

[1] Friedman's methodological approach is well illustrated by the now famous example: that of predicting the shots made by an expert billiard player. That is, one can predict such shots by assuming that the player behaved as if he / she knew and applied the mathematical formulas consistent with producing the shots generated on average by an expert player.

at the expense of more morally preferable alternatives. However, the lens of neoclassical economic theory is distorting practical realities.

The notion of *Homo economicus*, the standard model of the individual in economic theory, seems to be endangered in the social domain.*Homo economicus* comes to a choice situation with exogenously given preferencesover goods and actions.*Homo economicus* is endowed with effortlessly error-free cognition, and simply understands his / her own preferences.*Homo economicus* cares about his / her own material well-being. Self-regarding preferences are the essence of *homo economicus*. *Homo economicus*has no moral compunction. *Homo economicus* is outcome-orientedrather than process-oriented. *Homo economicus*acts in terms of the results of the actual choices the agent makes, anddoes not care about the manner in which the agent in question and others behave. The standard model assumes that people interact with each other in ways that are relatively frictionless and thus yield equilibriumbehavior. Finally, *Homo economicus* has a rate of time preference that allows him / her to allocate consumption over time in a consistent manner. Preferences are thus assumed not to change substantially over time, nor to be very different between wealthy and poor individuals, or even between individuals in different societies and cultures.

Behavioral economics aims to study how flesh-and-blood people act.What is important in behavioral economics is the appreciation of the realism of behavioral assumptions in terms of psychological, sociological, and institutional dimensions. There is an increasing recognition that these dimensions affect economic outcomes. It is important to understand how people behave with regard to both their cognitive abilities and their environmental conditions.One of the key messages of behavioral economics is that context matters in ways that are not recognized in standard economic modeling. Standard economic theory presumes that the way in which a situation is described does not (and should not) affect the preferences that people have. This "invariance"principle is a fundamental element of rationality (Arrow, 1982). Invariance is essential for the normative economic theory because violations of this principle imply that people do not have stable preferences. Some argue that the concept of *Homo economicus*is too narrow. People often repeat the same mistakes. Individuals are hyperbolic discounters, rather than exponential ones, of benefits and costs that accrue in the future. People are often driven by social norms. Though neoclassical economic theory assumes that people maximize utility, it postulates nothing about what utility is.Human beings do not know all of the alternatives that are available for action, and they are unable to make the calculations that would support optimization.One can discover the "intelligence" underlying choice behavior even if this behavior is not maximizing from the perspective of economic efficiency in the traditional sense. Rationality can be defined in terms of the process employed to make a decision, whether or not it happens to lead to the optimal outcomes. It is important to specify institutional constraints in which economic agents behave "rationally" broadly defined.

Generally speaking, the idea of institutions is understood as systems of established and prevalent social rules that structure social interactions (North, 1990). Institutional variations, as codified in social structures, create differing environments for the resolution of public issues in which the role of corporations in society is under debate. Bowles (2004) aims to offer a real departure from the neoclassical paradigm. Bowles primarily focuses on institutions. He defines institutions as "the laws, informal rules, and conventions that give a durable structure to social interactions among the members of a population" (2004, pp.47–48). He presents the following three approaches to illustrate fundamental questions about the role of institutions:

- *Non-contractual social interactions.* People are not always be regulated by a complete and readily enforced contract. Non-contractual social interactions take place in real life. Non-contractual aspects of interactions are governed by a combination of norms and power.
- *Adaptive and other-regarding behaviors.* People acquire their behavioral responses in part by copying the behaviors of those who they perceive as successful by some standard or by acting to maximize one's gains given one's beliefs about how others will act. Behavioral responses acquired by agents in one environment are unlikely to be acquired by the same agents were they to be functioning in an entirely different environment. Moreover, though self-interest is a powerful motive, other-regarding motives are also important in experiments and in natural settings.
- *Generalized increasing returns.* Social interactions often lead to patterns of what are called "positive feedbacks." Positive feedbacks create economic environments in which small chance events have durable consequences in the long-run (path-dependency). Institutional complementarities may generate generalized increasing returns. Generalized increasing returns due to these synergies appear to be a source of multiple equilibria.

The institutions governing a particular interaction will affect the preferences and beliefs of the participants. In making strategic decisions, it is important that a player consider the likely behavior of other players because the optimal actions of a player are positively related to the actions of the other players. Such strategic complementarity between individual actions necessitates that players coordinate their decisions to reach efficient outcomes. Yet, decision makers typically fail to coordinate, that is, players do not select the equilibrium that yields the highest payoff from the set of available equilibria. Institutions also influence the distribution of information, the way in which information can be acquired, hidden, shared, and used. Different institutions give rise to distinct patterns of conflicts of interest among agents whose interdependence is not governed by complete contracts. Choosing the right institutions can improve efficiency by reducing conflicts of interest over non-contractual elements of transactions.

Social norms are a widely used concept for explaining human behavior. Culture shapes our daily behaviors, guiding much of what we do and do not by prescribing what behavior is acceptable. Social norms are the result of social learning, and a particular behavior would become prevalent in a population.Under conformist transmission, individuals preferentially adopt the common behavior, which increases its frequency in the population. Individuals living in the same group tend to behave in similar ways, holding the same beliefs and values, whereas people living in different groups tend to think and behave differently. Such beliefs and values are transmitted within social groups by various forms of social learning. In humans, social learning gives rise to cumulative cultural change not seen in other animals. Once there exist differences between cultural groups, there is selection pressure in favor of the persistence and proliferation of those cultural traits that are broadly "pro-social." A cultural environment is any social situation affecting the propensity of existing cultural traits to be adopted and retained by others and new cultural traits to be introduced.

According to Leibenstein (1979), the micro-micro problem is the study of what goes on inside a "black box." He argued that conventional micro theory is based on a theory of single person behavior. His approach aims to explain organizations' external activities through study of their internal processes. It is common in neoclassical economics to assume that effort is maximized in its quantity and quality dimensions irrespective of institutional conditions. However, Leibenstein's theory of x-efficiency poses a problem for studies of effort variability and emphasizes the importance of interaction between patterns of production and worker morale. X-efficient production represents the maximum level of output that can be realized by utility-maximizing agents. According to the theory of x-efficiency, effort is a discretionary variable in the production process and is affected by the environment. X-inefficiency can be defined as differences in productivity between what can be achieved when economic agents supply effort in an ideal environment and what is supplied in a sub-optimal environment. Economic agents are not all the same and therefore characterized by different objective functions. Whether x-efficiency is achieved or not depends on the economic agents' preferences. Moreover, the introduction of effort discretion into the modeling of the path dependency theory allows for the persistence of multiple (optimal and sub-optimal) equilibria. It helps to explain the development of inefficient economic regimes. X-inefficiency–the deviation of labor productivity from its maximum–can exist under competitive conditions.Within the firm and the household, Leibenstein considered personal motivations and interpersonal relations.

We can show intrapersonal tensions in economic models. Economic theory considers the concept of self in the following two cases: the problem of self-control in decision making and the problem of decision making which is extended to the role of self-image. In the former case, the self appears as a decision maker who is biased by psychological features such as the tendency to procrastinate and the drive to addiction. In the latter case, self-image regards the self taken as an object. Individuals can be single persons, groups of people, and the different selves of single persons.

Our first objective is to view intertemporal choice as the outcome of a conflict between multiple selves.People are more impatient when they make short-run tradeoffs than when they make long-run tradeoffs. This creates a conflict between an economic agent's preferences at different points in time: the course of action preferred today by a hyperbolic agent does not coincide with the one he / she would like to implement tomorrow. The behavior of individuals systematically discount the future relative to the present more heavily than they would themselves like. Individuals do things they would not have done if they had made the decision to act from a remote perspective, and they do not follow their own plans. Although people initially decide to take a far-sighted course of action, they subsequently succumb to temptation. Hyperbolic discounting transforms a unitary self into a population of competing selves. The self is a dynamic and ever-changing entity over time. As a result, self-control and the degree to which individuals are able to commit to future choices become crucial issues for decision making. Self-control can be defined as efforts made by the individual to avoid or resist behaving inconsistently.People may decide how much to save in a variety of ways that are susceptible to behavioral factors. Although people have preferences for saving in order to have a smooth consumption stream, they also have preferences for immediate gratification. Time inconsistent consumers may formulate the same future saving plan as a conventional life-cycle planner, but engage in short-term behavior that violates the plan.

Our second objective is to discuss identity in economics. A single person can have different selves as a person's different social identities. Social identities are based on group membership. Concerning utility, an individual's identity describes gains and losses in utility from behavior that conforms or departs from the norms for particular social categories in particular situations.Values are held in common by community members. Different persons can make up a single social group as their shared social identity. The contemporary world in which we find ourselves is characterized by interpretations of norms and, more generally, cultural factors. Cultural factors have a determining influence on individual's cognitive processes. People experience culture as schematic structures that organize that information. Differences in norms tied to social identities help explain differences in economic outcomes.We develop a theory of oppositional cultures. An oppositional culture is a minority of a population with norms and beliefs that differ from the norms and beliefs of the majority. Coordination requires an additional cost if the agent has to change cultures. Effort is not subject to contract. Given effort variability, different coordination costs can generate different effort levels among firms. There are effort complementarities between the parties, which enforces a multiplicity of possible equilibrium outcomes.

Our third objective is to discuss possible selves in economics.People have an array of possible selves. The self-system is multifaceted and dynamic, with different self-representations activated at different times. The future self may be different from the current self as information and needs change. People are subject to some bias, failing to adjust properly for possible information with different backgrounds. Bias takes the shape of an image conceived and standardized by individuals belonging to one culture.The possible selves construct offers a detailed description of future-oriented self-representations. The construct is linked to motivation and behavior through the process of self-regulation. Comparison between the actual self and the ideal self has important motivational consequences. The response to perceived discrepancy can be shaped toward desired behavioral change. However, self-verification is also an important factor in the individual's motivational system. Self-verification is expected to undermine intentional self-change. Individuals may have an inert area within which they do not attempt self-change. The inert area idea permits both optimal and sub-optimal economic outcomes within the same model.

Our last objective is to analyze how individuals can acquire and internalize their norms through socialization. Economic behavior can be described as either altruistic or envious. Diverse morale and the evolution of norms interact in nontrivial ways. The intuition behind complements can be extended to strategic contexts. When choices are complements, then self-regarding (or other-regarding) agents may have an incentive to mimic the behavior of other-regarding (or self-regarding) agents. The process by which norms evolve exhibits generalized increasing returns. There are two steady states with different effort levels. If the norm, which is enforced by altruism, persists in the limit, everyone chooses the high effort level and high morale is sustainable. On the other hand, if the norm, which is enforced by envy, is persistent, everyone chooses the low effort level and the performance decays in the long run. Therefore, there are situations in which other-regarding (or self-regarding) preferences may dominate the outcome of social interactions. This multiplicity can explain why economic performance varies across societies. Conformity with social norms will be self-enforcing in the presence of multiple equilibria.

REFERENCES

Ainslie, G. (1975). Specious reward: a behavioral theory of impulsiveness and impulse control. *Psychological Bulletin*, *82*, 463–496.

Ainslie, G. (2001). *Breakdown of Will*. Cambridge: Cambridge University Press.

Akerlof, G.A. (1980). A theory of social customs, of which unemployment may be one consequence. *Quarterly Journal of Economics*,*94*, 749– 775.

Akerlof, G.A. (1991). Procrastination and obedience.*American Economic Review*, *81*, 1–19.

Akerlof, G.A. (1997). Social distance and social decisions. *Econometrica*, *65*, 1005– 1027.

Akerlof, G.A. & Kranton, R.E. (2000). Economics and identity. *Quarterly Journal of Economics*, *115*, 715–753.

Akerlof, G.A. & Kranton, R.E. (2002). Identity and schooling: some lessons for the economics of education. *Journal of Economic Literature*, *40*, 1167–1201.

Akerlof, G.A. & Kranton, R.E. (2005). Identity and the economics of organizations. *Journal of Economic Perspectives*, *19*, 9–32.

Altman, M.(2000). A behavioral model of path dependency: the economics of profitable inefficiency and market failure. *Journal of Socio-Economics*,*29*, 127–145.

Altman, M. (2001). Culture, human agency, and economic theory: culture asa determinant of material welfare. *Journal of Socio-Economics*,*30*,379–391.

Altman, M. (2005). The ethical economy and competitive markets: reconciling altruistic, moralistic, and ethical behavior with the rational economic agent and competitive markets. *Journal of Economic Psychology*, *26*, 732–757.

Arrow, K.J. (1982). Risk perception in psychology and economics. *Economic Inquiry*, *20*, 1–9.

Arthur, W.B. (1994). *Increasing Returns and Path Dependency in the Economy*. Ann Arbor: University of Michigan Press.

Axelrod, R. (1997). The dissemination of culture: a model with local convergence and global polarization. *Journal of Conflict Resolution, 41*, 203- 226.

Bardsley, N.&Sugden, R. (2006). Human nature and sociality in economics. In Kolm, S.-Ch., &Ythier, J.M. (Eds), *Handbook of the Economics of Giving, Altruism and Reciprocity: Foundations, Volume 1* (731–768). Amsterdam, The Netherlands: North-Holland.

Barro, R. (1974). Are government bonds net wealth? *Journal of Political Economy, 82*, 1095–1117.

Becker, G. S. (1976). Altruism, egoism, and genetic fitness: economics and sociobiology. *Journal of Economic Literature, 4*, 817–826.

Becker, G.S. &Murphy, K.M. (1988). A theory of rational addiction. *Journal of PoliticalEconomy*, *96*, 675–700.

Bénabou, R. &Tirole, J. (2002). Self-confidence and personal motivation. *Quarterly Journal of Economics*, *117*, 871–915.

Bénabou, R. &Tirole, J. (2004). Willpower and personal rules. *Journal of Political Economy*, *112*, 848–886.

Ben-Ner, A. &Putterman, L. (2000). On some implications of evolutionary psychology for the study of preferences and institutions. *Journal of Economic Behavior and Organization, 43*, 91–99.

Bernheim, B.D. (1994). A theory of conformity.*Journal of Political Economy, 102*, 841- 877.

Bergstrom, T. C.& Stark, O. (1993). How altruism can prevail in an evolutionary environment. *American Economic Review, 83*, 149–155.

Bester, H. &Güth, W. (1998). Is altruism evolutionarily stable? *Journal of Economic Behavior and Organization, 34,* 193–209.

Bisin, A. &Verdier, T. (2001). The economics of cultural transmission and the dynamics of preferences. *Journal of Economic Theory*, *97*, 298–319.

Bowles, S. (1998). Endogenous preferences: the cultural consequences of markets and other economic institutions. *Journal of Economic Literature,36*, 75–111.

Bowles, S. (2004). *Microeconomics: Behavior, Institutions, and Evolution.* Princeton:Princeton University Press.

Bowles, S. &Gintis, H. (2000). Walrasian economics in retrospect. *QuarterlyJournal of Economics, 115*, 1411–1439.

Camerer, C. F. (2003). *Behavioral Game Theory: Experiments in Strategic Interaction.* Princeton: PrincetonUniversity Press.

Camerer, C.F. & Fehr, E. (2006). When does "Economic Man" dominate socialbehavior? *Science,311*, 47–52.

Charness, G. &Rabin, M. (2002). Understanding social preferences with simple tests. *Quarterly Journal of Economics,117*, 817–869.

Compte, O. &Postlewaite, A. (2004). Confidence-enhanced performance. *American Economic Review, 94*, 1536–1557

Denzau, A.T. &North, D.C. (1994). Shared mental models: ideologies and institutions. *Kyklos. 47*, 3–31.

Diamond, P. &Köszegi, B. (2003). Quasi-hyperbolic discounting and retirement. *Journal of Public Economics, 87*, 1839–1872.

DiMaggio, P. (1997). Culture and cognition. *Annual Review of Sociology,23*, 263– 287.

Elster, J. (1998). Emotions and economic theory.*Journal of Economic Literature,36*, 47–74.

Fehr, E., Fischbacher, U. &Kosfeld, M. (2005). Neuroeconomic foundations of trust and social preferences: initial evidence. *American Economic Review, 95*, 346–351.

Fehr, E., Kirchsteiger, G. &Riedl, A. (1993). Does fairness prevent market clearing? an experimental investigation. *Quarterly Journal of Economics, 108*, 437–459.

Fehr, E. & Schmidt, K.M. (1999). A theory of fairness, competition, and cooperation. *Quarterly Journal of Economics, 114*, 817–868.

Frank, R. (1988). *Passions within Reason: the Strategic Role of the Emotions.* New York:Norton.

Freeman, E. (1984). *Strategic Management: A Stakeholder Approach.*Boston: Pitman Publishing.

Friedman, M. (1953). *Essays in Positive Economics.* Chicago: University of Chicago Press.

Friedman, M. (1962). *Capitalism and Freedom.*Chicago: University of Chicago Press.

Fudenberg, D. & Levine, D.K. (2006). A dual-self model of impulse control. *American Economic Review, 96*, 1449–1476.

Geanakoplos, J., Pearce, D. & Stacchetti, E. (1989). Psychological games and sequential rationality. *Games and Economic Behavior, 1*, 60–79.

Gintis, H. (2003). The hitchhiker's guide to altruism: gene-culture coevolution, and the internalization of norms. *Journal of Theoretical Biology, 220*, 407–418.

Gintis, H. (2007). A framework for the unification of the behavioral sciences. *Behavioral and Brain Sciences, 30*, 1–61.

Gintis, H., Henrich, J., Bowles, S., Boyd, R.& Fehr, E. (2008). Strong reciprocity and the roots of human morality. *Social Justice Research, 21*, 241–253.

Gruber, J. &Köszegi, B. (2001). Is addiction "rational"? theory and evidence. *Quarterly Journal of Economics, 116*, 1261–1303.

Gul, F. &Pesendorfer, W. (2001). Temptation and self-control. *Econometrica, 69*, 1403–1435.

Güth, W., Schmittberger, R., &Schwarze, R. (1982). An experimental analysis of ultimatum bargaining. *Journal of Economic Behavior and Organization, 3*, 367–388.

Harris, M. (1975). *Culture, People, Nature: An Introduction to General Anthropology*. New York: Thomas Y. Crowell Company.

Henrich, J. (2000). Does culture matter in economic behavior? ultimatum game bargaining among the Machiguenga of the Peruvian Amazon. *American Economic Review, 90*, 973–979.

Henrich, M. (2004). Cultural group selection, coevolutionary processes and large-scale cooperation. *Journal of Economic Behavior and Organization, 53*, 3–35.

Henrich, J. Boyd, R., Bowles, S., Camerer, C., Fehr, E., Gintis, H. &McElreach, R. (2001). In search of Homo economicus: behavioral experiments in 15 small-scale societies. *American Economic Review, 91*, 75–78.

Higgins, E.T. (1987). Self-discrepancy: a theory relating self and affect. *Psychological Review, 94*, 319–340.

Hume, D. (1739–40 [1985]). *A Treatise of Human Nature*. London: Penguin Books.

Isaac, R.M. & Walker, J.M. (1988). Group size effects in public goods provision: the voluntary contribution mechanism. *Quarterly Journal of Economics,103*, 179–200.

Kahneman, D. (2003). Maps of bounded rationality: psychology for behavioral economics. *American Economic Review, 93*, 1449–1475.

Kahneman, D., Knetsch, J.L.&Thaler, R. (1986). Fairness as a constraint on profit seeking: entitlements in the market. *American Economic Review, 76*, 728–741.

Kahneman, D. &Thaler, R.H. (2006). Anomalies: utility maximization and experienced utility. *Journal of Economic Perspectives, 20*, 221–234.

Kahneman, D. &Tversky, A. (1974). Judgment under uncertainty: heuristics and biases. *Science, 185*, 1124–1131.

Kahneman, D. &Tversky, A. (1979). Prospect theory: an analysis of decision under risk. *Econometrica, 47*, 263–291.

Kan, K. (2007). Cigarette smoking and self-control. *Journal of Health Economics, 26*, 61–81.

Kaufman, B. (1999). Emotional arousal as a source of bounded rationality. *Journal of Economic Behavior and Organization, 38*, 135–144.

Khalil, E. L. (2004). What is altruism? *Journal of Economic Psychology, 25*, 97–123.

Kirby, K.N. & Herrnstein, R.J. (1995). Preference reversals due to myopic discounting of delayed rewards. *Psychological Science, 6*, 83–89.

Laibson, D. (1997). Golden eggs and hyperbolic discounting. *Quarterly Journal of Economics, 112*, 443–477.

Lazear, E.P. (1999). Culture and language. *Journal of Political Economy, 107*, S95–S126.

Lea, S. &Webley, P. (2005). In search of the economic self. *Journal of Socio-Economics, 34*, 585–604.

Leary, M.R. (1995). *Self-Presentation: Impression Management and Interpersonal Behavior*. Boulder: Westview Press.

Leibenstein, H. (1966). Allocative efficiency vs. 'X-efficiency'. *American Economic Review, 56*, 392–415.

Leibenstein, H.(1979). A branch of economics is missing: micro-microtheory. *Journal of Economic Literature, 17*, 477–502.

Leibenstein, H. (1987). *Inside the Firm: The Inefficiencies of Hierarchy*. Cambridge: Harvard University Press.

Liebowitz, S.J. & Margolis, S.E. (1990). The fable of the keys. *Journal of Law and Economics, 33*, 1–25.

Liebowitz, S.J. & Margolis, S.E. (1994). Network externalities: an uncommon tragedy. *Journal of Economic Perspectives,33*, 133–150.

Lester, D. (2003). Comment on "The self as a problem": alternative conceptions of the multiple self. *Journal of Socio-Economics, 32*, 499–502.

Lévy-Garboua, L., Meidinger, C.&Rapoport, B. (2006). The formation of social preferences: some lessons from psychology and biology. In Kolm, S.-Ch., &Ythier, J.M. (Eds), *Handbook of the Economics of Giving, Altruism and Reciprocity: Foundations, Volume 1* (545–613). Amsterdam, The Netherlands: North-Holland.

Lewis, D. (1969 [2002]). *Convention: A Philosophical Study.*Oxford: Basil Blackwell.

Loewenstein, G. (1987). Anticipation and the value of delayed consumption. *EconomicJournal*, *97*, 666–684.

Loewenstein, G. (1996). Out of control: visceral influences on behavior. *Organizational Behavior and Human Decision Processes,65*, 272–297.

Markus, H. &Nurius, P. (1986). Possible selves. *American Psychologists, 41*, 954–969.

Maynard Smith, J. (1982). *Evolution and the Theory of Games.* Cambridge: CambridgeUniversity Press.

Moldoveanu, M. & Stevenson, H. (2001). The self as a problem: the intra-personal coordination of conflicting desires. *Journal of Socio-Economics, 30*, 295–330.

North, D.C. (1990). *Institutions, Institutional Change, and Economic Performance.* Cambridge: Cambridge University Press.

North, D.C. (2005). *Understanding the Process of Economic Change.* Princeton: Princeton University Press.

O'Donoghue, T. & Rabin, M. (1999a). Doing it now or later. *American Economic Review*, *89*, 103–124.

O'Donoghue, T. & Rabin, M. (1999b). Incentives for procrastinators. *Quarterly Journal of Economics*, *114*, 769–816.

O'Donoghue, T. & Rabin, M. (2001). Choice and procrastination. *Quarterly Journal of Economics*, *116*, 121–160.

Pecchenino, R.A. (2009). Becoming: identity and spirituality. *Journal of Socio-Economics*, *38*, 31–36.

Phelps, E.S. &Pollak, R.A. (1968). On second-best national saving and game - equilibrium growth. *Reviewof Economic Studies*, *35*, 185–199.

Rabin, M. (1993). Incorporating fairness into game theory and economics. *American Economic Review, 83*, 1281–1302.

Rabin, M. (1998). Psychology and economics. *Journal of Economic Literature*, *36*, 11–46.

Roth, A., Prasnikar, V., Okuno-Fujiwara, M.&Zamir, S. (1991). Bargaining and market behavior in Jerusalem, Ljubljana, Pittsburgh, and Tokyo: an experimental study. *American Economic Review, 81*, 1068–1095.

Samuelson, P.A. (1937). A note on measurement of utility. *Review of Economic Studies*, *4*, 155–161.

Simon, H.A. (1959). Theories of decision making in economics and behavioral science.*American Economic Review, 49,* 252–283.

Simon, H.A. (1978). Rationality as a process and as a product of thought. *American Economic Review, 70,* 1–16.

Simon, H.A. (1993). Altruism and economics. *American Economic Review, 83*, 156–161.

Smith, A. (1759 [1976]). *The Theory of Moral Sentiments*. Indianapolis: Liberty Classics.

Smith, V.L. (2003). Constructivist and ecological rationality in economics. *American Economic Review, 93*, 465–508.

Stroz, R.H. (1956). Myopia and inconsistency in dynamic utility maximization. *Reviewof Economic Studies*, *23*, 165–180.

Sugden, R. (2005). Fellow-feeling. In Gui, B., &Sugden, R. (Eds), *Economics and Social Interaction* (52–75). Cambridge: Cambridge University Press.

Swann, W. B. Jr., Stein-Seroussi, A. &Giesler, B. (1992). Why people self-verify. *Journal of Personality and Social Psychology*, *62*, 392–401.

Teraji, S. (2007). Morale and the evolution of norms. *Journal of Socio-Economics*, *36*, 48–57.

Teraji, S. (2008). Culture, effort variability, and hierarchy. *Journal of Socio-Economics*, *37*, 157–166.

Teraji, S. (2009). The economics of possible selves. *Journal of Socio-Economics*, *38*, 45–51.

Thaler, R.H. (2000). From Homo Economicus to Homo Sapiens. *Journal of Economic Perspectives*, *14*, 133–141.

INDEX

F

G

H

I

J

K

L

M

N

O

W

X